LAZARIS

LAZARIS INTERVIEWS
BOOK II

CONCEPT: SYNERGY PUBLISHING

Who is Lazaris?

Lazaris is a nonphysical entity. He is a consciousness without form — a Spark of Light, a Spark of Love — an energy that has never chosen to take human form. He is most frequently known as "the one who waits for us at the edge of our reality."

Lazaris is wise beyond what we have known, loving beyond what we have conceived, and committed to each of us in our search for enlightenment. He is a delightful friend — a gentle and powerful guide for our Spiritual Journey Home to God/Goddess/All That Is.

The way that Lazaris communicates to us is called channeling — in this case Objective, Full-Trance Channeling. That means several things. "Objective" means that Lazaris is not a part of the consciousness of his channel. "Full Trance" means that the channel (Jach Pursel) is not aware of what is being said during the trance state. "Channeling" is perhaps best described by Lazaris directly:

"In order to communicate with you, we send forth a series of vibrations. These vibratory frequencies go through a series of 'step-down generations' until they can safely enter your reality.

"The energy field of the one you call Jach acts like an antenna; his body, like an amplifier. The vibration we create in our reality is thus amplified in your reality. Your ears and eyes pick up those amplified frequencies and translate them into sounds — you hear a voice — and pictures — you see animation.

"When we communicate we are not in the body — how archaic! Such behavior is no more necessary than having your nightly newscaster actually be in your television set!

"We keep the channel in a sleep-like state so that he stays out of the way. It would be possible for him to 'witness' what we say — to 'listen' as the vibrations go by — but we prefer him to be completely out of the way. The best way to keep the information pure is to have the channel be as much a 'pure instrument' as possible."

Lazaris is a channeled entity, but he is so very much more. Many who are familiar with metaphysics and channeling say, "There is channeling, and then there is Lazaris. He is so far beyond ... he stands alone in this field."

Lazaris...

Lazaris says he came not as a guru, but as a friend. I've found that what I value most I've learned from friends, and Lazaris is one of the best friends I have.

— *Colin Higgins, Writer/Director, "Harold & Maude," "Silver Streak," "Foul Play," "The Best Little Whorehouse in Texas," "Nine to Five"*

Lazaris represents the Highest Self of humanity. When one is in communication with him it activates that Highest Self in that person. Lazaris' energy literally magnetizes that Highest Self to be experienced as real, as who we really are. It is a privilege and vital opportunity to communicate with this level of consciousness.

— *Barbara Marx Hubbard, Futurist*

Lazaris is the friend we always wish for, and now he's here for everyone. We had a good relationship before, but he showed us how to love each other even more. We always thought that success came after long and hard work. Lazaris taught us it's more fun to do it quicker and easier. With Lazaris' love and help we have created one miracle after another.

— *Renée Taylor & Joe Bologna, Actors, Writers & Directors*

With wisdom, compassion and marvelous humor, Lazaris, from his greater perspective outside our "Set," makes vividly clear how physical reality works. He knows me absolutely and is there for me — even when I am not! Thank you, Lazaris. I love you. . . .

— *Betty Fuller, Director, The Trager Institute*

I went to Lazaris' first public channeling in 1979. Since that day the quality of information and communication has always expanded and surpassed itself. The growth I have made because of our friendship has brought me into the New Age with clarity and assurance. I love Lazaris even more today and rejoice in our shared vision for the exciting future!

— *Nicholas Eliopoulos, Producer/Director/Writer, and Emmy Award-winning Editor for "Wallenberg: A Hero's Story," Senior Vice President of Development/ Production, The Don Johnson Company*

Lazaris, it's magic! It is magic! Thank you, Lazaris, for showing me how to pull rabbits out of hats!

—*Sharon Gless, "Cagney & Lacey"*

LAZARIS

LAZARIS INTERVIEWS BOOK II

CONCEPT: SYNERGY PUBLISHING

Lazaris

Lazaris Interviews, Book II

1st Printing, 1988
© *1988 Concept: Synergy Publishing, 279 S. Beverly Drive, Suite 604,*
Beverly Hills, CA 90212, 213/285-1507

Cover photograph by Michaell North
ISBN 1-55638-090-9, Library of Congress Catalog Card Number 88-070670
Printed in the United States of America
10 9 8 7 6 5 4 3 2 1

Dedication

This book is dedicated to Peny,
the one we came to touch,
the one who truly touches us.
We love you.

—Lazaris

Books by Lazaris

A Note on Lazaris' Use of Language ...

Throughout this book Lazaris refers to himself as "we". Ever since he began communicating with us in 1974, he has done that. Lazaris says that each of us has many "selves," but that right now we are experiencing them "one at a time," and thus refer to ourselves as "I". Lazaris has many selves as well — many selves in many dimensions — but experiences them all simultaneously, and therefore refers to himself as "we". It is not the use of the "royal we," but rather Lazaris' experience of his own reality. ...

Also, often you will find that Lazaris will use a plural pronoun in a place you might expect to find a singular one. This is to avoid using the generic masculine pronouns which tend to make women feel as though they are not included in what is being said. To make certain they do know they are included, Lazaris often uses plural pronouns which, though "against the rules," are better aligned with what is true.

Contents

Acknowledgements

This book is made up of a number of interviews, and in addition incorporates the questions and answers from the Evenings with Lazaris which have followed Weekends with Lazaris (two-day seminars). Following each question is a line that identifies the publication and the interviewer who asked the question — or the workshop at which the question was asked. In the case where there are several consecutive questions from the same interview, the identifying line follows the answer to the last question in the series.

Lazaris and Concept: Synergy gratefully acknowledge and thank the following people and publications for their participation in generating the material for this book:

Craig Steele, *Together Bookstore Monthly Newsletter*, Together Books, 2220 E. Colfax Avenue, Denver, CO 80206.

Paul Zuromski, *Body, Mind & Spirit Magazine*, P. O. Box 701, Providence, RI 02901.

Craig Lee, *LA Weekly*, 2140 Hyperion Avenue, Los Angeles, CA 90027, used by permission.

Mary Ellen Pratt and Jack Clarke, *New Age Information Network*, P. O. Box 566714, Atlanta, Georgia, 30356.

Patricia Clay, *Infinite Thought*, Son-Light Publications, P. O. Box 82525, San Diego, CA 92138-2525.

David Rogers, *Llewellyn's New Times*, 213 E. Fourth St., St. Paul, Minnesota, 55101.

Brian Williams, *Unicorn*, P. O. Box 431, Paddington (Brisbane), Queensland, Australia 4064.

Van Ault, *Magical Blend Magazine*, P. O. Box 11303, San Francisco, CA 94101.

E. James Faubel, *Transformation Times*, P. O. Box 425, Beaver Creek, Oregon 97004.

Lawrence Stoller, The Crystal Congress, P. O. Box 5442, Mill Valley, California 94942.

Marilyn Ferguson, *Brain/Mind Bulletin*, P. O. Box 42211, Los Angeles, California 90042.

Lee Perry, 17510 Sherman Way, #212, Van Nuys, California 91406.

Cindy Saul, *PhenomeNEWS*, 28545 Greenfield, Suite 111, Southfield, Michigan 48076.

Cathy Lester, *New Orleans Resources*, 8237 Apricot Street, New Orleans, Louisiana 70118.

Murray Needleman, Psychologist, *The Murray Needleman Show*, WWDB-FM Radio, Philadelphia, PA 19131, used by permission.

Merv Griffin, *The Merv Griffin Show*, by permission of Merv Griffin Enterprises, 1541 N. Vine Street, Hollywood, CA 90028.

Alan Vaughan, *Whole Life Monthly*, 509 Santa Monica Blvd., Suite 212, Santa Monica, CA 90401.

Brian Enright and Lisa Michelle Guest, *Los Angeles and Orange County Resources*, published by Community Resource Publications, 228 - 20th St., Huntington Beach, CA 92648.

Victoria Fugit, *The Catalyst*, 140 S. McClelland, Salt Lake City, UT 84102.

Penny Price, *A Complete Guide to Channeling*, Penny Price Productions, 670 El Media Avenue, Pacific Palisades, CA 90272, used by permission.

The participants of the Seattle, Philadelphia and Atlanta Evenings with Lazaris who asked anonymous questions that became a part of this book.

We would also like to thank Michaell North (for his cover photograph of Jach) and Norman Seeff for the photographs of Lazaris and Jach Pursel that are found in the body of this book.

A special thank you to Zoë Landers and Morgaan Sinclair for their valuable and consistent help in putting this book together.

Introductions

Introduction

by Jach Pursel

I still remember the first meditation. The path twisted this way and that. Green … everything so very green. The ferns, tall. Trees, lush. Sweet smells. So engrossed in the detail, I forgot to be startled. I forgot to disbelieve.

The images burst. My mind raced ahead. I kept following. Then I saw an intriguing cabin. "Oh, brother," I thought. "This is just too corny! This is almost embarrassing!" But there was something different about this particular cabin. The spontaneity and the uniqueness silenced my skepticism and my sarcasm.

Surrounded in tall pines and sequoias, it had a thatched roof and sparkling glass windows with diamond-shaped beveled panes. The exterior walls were rough cut, but the slightly ajar door was smooth and finely crafted. It was certainly "Americana," but it was something else as well. It intrigued me. It welcomed me.

Maybe it was the twill of smoke. Perhaps it was the warmth of the light pouring from windows and door. The details astonished me. The racing stopped.

I stood for a very long time. Inching my way, the path gave way to three steps. I finally crossed the porch and reached for the latch. The door opened on its own. My skepticism bubbled briefly. I could almost hear it breathe. I stepped into the room.

A man was standing in front of me. He was gentle. I was not afraid. He spoke to me. I remembered every word. Our relationship began ...

Now, so many years later, I see Lazaris as the spark of love and light that he more correctly is. When I need answers to specific questions, I give Peny a list and she records or notes the responses during her next private time with Lazaris.

Sometimes I need the feeling of Lazaris more than the facts of his answers. When I want to just be with Lazaris, I return to that "almost embarrassing," but very real, place. Each time, I repeat the steps. Each time, I reach for the latch, and the door opens by itself. Each time.

Lazaris is always there for me. He is always there. During these feeling times, I don't ask anything. I sit with Lazaris. His energy envelopes me. I let him embrace me with his love, his caring, and his intimacy. I experience his compassion. I experience beyond the words that he might speak. I experience Lazaris.

I needed one of those feeling times when Lazaris decided to make video tapes. Prior to November, 1985, Lazaris had been talking with people privately and conducting afternoon workshops and weekend seminars. Though there were many thousands of people who participated in the consultations and the events, my experience of it all was still very personal and very private.

The release of video tapes and making the audio tapes available through bookstores and centers throughout the United States, Canada, Australia, and selected places in Europe and Asia, seemed too public — too visible. I sat with Lazaris. I stretched my image. I let in a little more of who Lazaris is and what he's about. I let him in. It became okay.

As I learn and grow with Lazaris — I listen to the tapes and take notes just like everyone else — those feeling times have become increasingly important. I sit with Lazaris for what seems like forever. Well, a very long time, at least. Then a rush of insight explodes inside of me. Gestalts seem to unfold spontaneously like fireworks on the Fourth of July. As abruptly, the experience ends. My eyes open. I have the sense of knowing. It's wonderful.

When it came time to decide whether to compile and release *Lazaris Interviews*, I needed one of those feeling times. Quite frankly, I had reservations.

Interview questions and answers are never intended to be a definitive exploration and explanation of a topic. The questions are pointed, and the answers are brief. What Lazaris would say to this question or that would not be his complete and total answer. Would people understand that? Would people mistakenly think this was all Lazaris had to say on a particular topic or issue? Would it be better to wait until Lazaris presented a fuller picture in a future book?

Due to the time/space considerations of the interview format, Lazaris answered questions as succinctly as possible. Would people mistake his brevity for shallowness?

When Lazaris does a workshop, he responds to the energy — the needs and wants — of the participants. When he responds to an interviewer, he answers in such a way that the questioner and audience will best understand — will best be able to relate to — what he's saying. How will regional questions and answers translate to a universal readership?

Many interviews ask the same questions. How can we keep the book from being redundant and still retain the integrity of each interview?

My mind raced with resistance. What format? Is it organized by interview or by topic? How do we decide which questions to include and which ones to leave out? How do we decide which repeated question goes in and which goes out? How ...? I was on a roll!

Finally I stopped and went to the feeling place with Lazaris. I sat. Oh, I wanted to argue and resolve all my "what if's" and "how about's." I sat. I let Lazaris in. I let him love me. In his way he told me: "Read it. Just read it."

That was it. Nothing profound. Or at least nothing that seemed profound at the time.

As the pieces of the books were fitted together, I began to read. It was very late one night — I tend to stay up very late since I spend so much time in trance. I run off the energy at three or four in the morning. I make up for the hours I spend in trance late at night when everyone else is sleeping. I began to read.

As I am reading, my mind flashes on that one evening back in 1976. It was very late then, too. I was all alone like I am now. The room was totally dark. Well, it's almost like that now. Then I was listening to a cassette tape; now I'm reading.

I remember. I was lying on the floor just listening. I was still amazed that that voice was coming out of my body. Now I am more used to it, though not totally. That night I just listened.

That night I heard the words, but I heard something more. It was something between the words. It was in the timbre, the cadence. It was in the urgency and the patience. I heard the love. That night, all alone, I heard the caring, the intimacy that Lazaris feels for each of us — for all of us. I heard the compassion.

Gripping the pages of manuscript, the same feeling washed over me. Tears once again rolled down my face. The tears gave way to sobs. Once again, I could feel Lazaris filling me with his incredible love and his soothing peace. I understood.

I could feel Lazaris in each answer I was reading, of course. More than that, I could feel Lazaris between the words. I could feel him in the style of response. I could feel him in each "we suggest" and in each "in that particular regard."

More importantly, people would feel that, too. Yes, the interviews would be read for information. More, the interviews would be read for their feeling and the understanding. The interviews would be read for the love, the light, the laughter, and the joy that is Lazaris.

Now I know why Lazaris said: "Read it. Just read it."

Enjoy for yourself. Let yourself learn. Let yourself experience the "feeling" time with Lazaris.

Jach Pursel
Los Angeles, March, 1988

From Lazaris ...

Well, all right. It is a pleasure to be working with you — it is a pleasure to be writing to you. Our purpose in communicating — in channeling our information — has been stated frequently. The media, many times intent upon being critical, has actually contributed to the dissemination of information more than it would like to admit.

You as individuals, as society, and as a humanity have decided to accelerate your growth and expand your awareness. You have asked for help.

More than ever, you are creating a Rubik's Cube-like reality where it seems like any one solution only leads to several more problems. The old answers born of linear problem solving simply do not work anymore. You have asked for new answers.

Our way of helping — our way of offering new answers — is to provide you with opportunity. Through exploration and examination we want to provide you the opportunity to encounter, unfold, befriend, and change your reality. We want to show you your actual old forms of reality creation and your potential new forms of future manifestation. We want to show you how to bridge from old to new.

If what you find in your exploration is detrimental, then we want to show you how to transmute and transform that energy into a power you can use to create a happier, more successful reality for yourself. We want to show you how to create a happier, more successful future for yourself and your world.

If what you discover augments who you are, we want to show you how to lift that awareness of self to a level of self-realization that can have a more profound, a more far-reaching impact upon you, your reality, and your future world.

With all the private consultations and workshop discussions, with all the meditations and Blendings, and with all the audio and video tapes, one of the common denominators is to consistently and continuously offer you the opportunity. Your opportunity.

Another common denominator is to offer you these opportunities via the means, the powerful means, of intimacy. The means matter. Ultimately the means are all that matter. Yes, we want to offer you opportunity, and it is critical to do it with intimacy.

Perhaps the most important reason we are communicating is the most personal reason: To communicate with Peny. Each day we speak together.

The content of our talks together varies broadly. Some evenings we review future workshops and seminars. We will often try out new techniques and meditations to make sure we are not "going too fast." Though we are never impatient, we are always enthusiastic — always eager.

Other times we work with Peny and her process and her programmings, though those times are less and less necessary. We spend time exploring philosophy and esoteric topics long into the night. Our energy combines with hers and we spiral beyond time and space on telepathic-like journeys. Then there are the times we laugh together and just have fun. Our relationship is truly one of loving friendship.

With the always changing form and context, our conversations may last hours or minutes. Most often the Channel's body is there in the gently darkened room, but, with all the travel, sometimes it's propped up on a hotel bed many miles away. Wherever his body is, our energy is always sitting quietly with Peny during our daily discussions.

What never changes is the intimacy Peny and we feel and actively create together. Friendship based on information and opportunity can be helpful — even valuable — but it will only last as long as the information and the opportunity is there. Such friendships, though wonderful, are linear.

The depth of friendship — the richness of friendship — the timelessness of friendship — the love of friendship — comes when the information and opportunity are blended with the magic of intimacy.

In our relationship with Peny, it is vital that we are close and tender and that we each actively create that closeness and tenderness. We softly speak of our love. Often.

Vulnerability and trust are integral parts of each of our interchanges together. Even at the height of the metaphysical circus and side show, our daily interactions became anchors of sensibilities: They reduced Peny's and the Channel's fear of humiliation.

Whether the conversation is profound or jocular, it is essential that the loving and caring be more than spoken. It is essential that it be demonstrated. Words can do more than just speak. Words can touch. Words can act. What gives them this life? The very love and care being expressed, if it's real. If it's real.

Intimacy is ultimately based on understanding. It is based on a desire to understand each other and a willingness to be understood.

For us, the *opportunity* of our relationship with Peny is the intimacy that we create with her. The *beauty* and the *wonder* of our relationship is the intimacy that she creates with us.

To you, Peny, *Lazaris Interviews* is like a remembrance of so many personal talks we have had together. Factually, the content and the context came from public interviews. Emotionally the meaning comes from many of our intimate talks with you.

To all of you, in *Lazaris Interviews* we answer a lot of different questions. The answers are intended to give you our point of view — to provide you with some information — to stimulate understanding and perception. More than the individual pieces of information and the opportunity they can encourage, the answers are intended to help you remember what you already know. The variety and brevity is intended to help you look beyond the information and to generate the intimacy that is there for you — that is waiting for you.

To each of you, we want to provide more than the *opportunity* to grow: We want to offer the *intimacy* of growing.

Peny, we thank you for the wonder and beauty of your love. We love you.

With Love and Peace ...

Lazaris

From Peny[*] ...

As we readied the interview books for printing, Lazaris asked me, as a favor to him, to share a piece of writing I did several years ago. I am usually reluctant to talk about my metaphysical experiences — it somehow seems trite these days to mention seeing ghosts, using telepathy, having out-of-body experiences, communicating with "dead" people — even the profound experiences with one's Higher Self are somehow becoming almost commonplace. I don't know quite what I think of all this yet.

At any rate, some close friends asked me to write a few lines about my spiritual odyssey, and I wrote this piece, in the third person. This piece primarily covers the time before Lazaris began channeling through Jach, which was October 3rd, 1974.

There had been a time when everything seemed like a brilliant confusion. Learning had always happened easily, and winning had always come almost as easily. Once a favorite teacher told her, "I feel sorry for you. Between your good luck and your high IQ, you'll never know the satisfaction of accomplishment over a difficult challenge."

Many of you have known Peny and Michaell as Peny and Michaell Prestini. For esoteric reasons they have changed their last name and now are Peny and Michaell North.

At this time the purpose of life seemed to be learning the rules and then realizing that you were expected to know when and how to modify the rules without getting caught. They had told her that the point of life was to be virtuous, **good**, and polite, and pray to Jesus ... and always to be the top of her class.

They hadn't realized that too often the intelligence it takes to always be the top will expose the stupidity of the moral philosophy they simultaneously hope to instill. And then the confusion escalates.

The confusion is long past now, and only rarely does a piece of it drift to shore again like a torn plank from a long-sunk galleon. Sometimes when she tried to explain how she got from there to here, the paradoxes and octave shifts and reality blends would get so entangled she'd want to just throw up her hands and laugh. How could she tell them that the way to get to the far shore might have to involve letting your initial vessel sink and then having to trust the sea goddess herself to transport you back to solid shifting sands?

The focus of her world now was love, and she fully realized the saccharine threat of trying to talk about it. She knew it was difficult for people to understand the love between herself and Michaell and Jach, but it was so alive and real and even flexible that they themselves regarded it as a conscious friend. And, shifting another few octaves, was the dyad love she shared with Michaell, a state of being that still made her catch her breath as she watched it grow and stretch like a sentient molecule realizing it can evolve into a star.

Everything in her life centered around this warm pyramid of love and the pyramid itself, like a candle-lit Bedouin tent in the black night desert, gave her courage and energy to meet the Universe and its Dance of Chaos head-on. She didn't care anymore about being the top or winning or even what others thought of her. She **did** care about the love, and, as for the rest of it, she found it difficult to explain.

How could she tell them that it really **is** only all illusion on this planet? And, worse yet, how could she tell them that the trick of handling the illusion is to concentrate on one piece at a time and change it before your very eyes, and **then** realize you can't pat yourself on the back because you only magically transformed an illusion! The problem didn't keep her worrying, though, because she had long since realized she didn't owe them anything, and she knew she'd only dance the dance as long as it was fun.

She remembered the strange period when she'd realized, past the point of refutation, that reality was an illusion done with holograms and mirrors. The freedom of the realization had quickly darkened with a sense of meaninglessness that crept across her playground like the lengthening shadow of twilight. For awhile it looked like the night would win; for awhile it looked like her entry into Chapel Perilous had finally over-extended her wherewithal.

She was well aware of her dilemma. She had finally gone too far. She had broken all the rules of censorship and restriction "for your own good" and, like an errant child catching daddy dress up as Santa Claus, she had stumbled onto the emptiest and freest of understandings — there's no one out there to rescue me.

The abyss offers no tour guides. You do your own research. So, she studied what she could find on the few who had stood there, and confusion almost ended the search. It was Blavatsky, of all the loving spirits, who finally forced her to see that there were only, after all, **two** options.

The cosmos supports simplicity without exception.

The options are layered in paradoxes so thick and convoluted that they end up looking identical at the surface. At the surface they both say "surrender." But underneath one lies sheer insanity — the insanity of giving away your power in order to have someone else do it all for you, the insanity of apathy and meaninglessness and eternal boredom and fear. That option has the prettiest facade, though, because it beckons you with pictures of idyllic childhood, and it is exceedingly tempting.

She had picked up this pretty little picture and considered signing up. She had stood there holding this tempting option like a beautiful music box begging to be listened to, and she had leaned out into the icy winds of conclusive evidence at the abyss and felt the pull of the yawning void, the space and shape of consciousness that is epitomized on the physical plane by the astronomical black holes of space. And just at the critical moment, when the first few notes of the **mechanical** music box reached her ears, she began to hum her own song instead ... and the lights switched on.

Sometime, if you care to ask, I'll tell you how she created a complex and very, very magical world full of present-tense activity. A world of art and books and music. A world of communicating with "dead" entities like Anäis Nin and Colette, a world of playing with long-forgotten goddesses like Isis and the Crone, a world of swirling creativity that clearly recognizes self-pity and boredom as the enemies and cheerfully reckons with them.

The "how" of it all is not as important as the "why," and she was extremely wary of anyone who told her not to ask "why." First you create the type of space you want to play in, and **then** you manifest the toys. Lazaris had told her that so many years ago, and she laughed with delight as she saw the space taking shape.

Sometimes, very late at night when she was having a session with Lazaris, she felt the love between them like sheer voltage, and she thanked herself again for setting that beautiful music box back down again at the edge of the abyss so long ago.

I love you.

Peny
Los Angeles, 1988

Lazaris Talks about Lazaris

On Not Being Physical

Q: I know you've answered this many times, but just for this particular piece: Have you ever been physical before or in a physical body?

Lazaris: No, we never have. We have made that decision, clearly, and we have existed without form. Many people on the East Coast and people on the West Coast often feel that there is nothing in between, yes? There's the East River, and then there's San Francisco and Los Angeles, or whatever.

You do, however, accept the possibility that there are people in the Midwest. You finally opened yourself up to that, yes? The thought that maybe some of those Midwesterners really do not ever care to go to the East Coast or the West Coast — that indeed they might well be happy living in the middle of Iowa and have no desire to travel anywhere else — is still a preponderance of wonder for many people.

Further, there are people in the middle of Iowa who can't fathom that anyone would prefer to be in New York or Los Angeles or San Francisco. They can't understand why everyone wouldn't want to live where they do.

So it is that you believe that since you are physical, everyone must have been physical, or at least wants to be. Open yourselves up to the possibility that there are those consciousnesses — and we would dare say that there are more of us than there are of you — that have decided: No, we don't particularly care to be physical, and we will never have the desire to do so. Now you're starting, as a humanity, to open up to that possibility, although it's still rather difficult for many people.

L azaris: To be physical or not is a decision process that everyone goes through. Every consciousness is first a spark of consciousness. In its process of growth, and in its decision to grow, in its desire to understand itself, and to become more of who it is, it has that option. Very early on, each decides to grow in a physical or in a nonphysical form.

Q: Why did you choose not to become physical? Why did you decide to become a teacher in this way?

You have chosen to do it physically. Subsequently, you answered thousands of other questions that rather led to the process of manifesting yourself on the Earth Plane in the numerous lifetimes that you have chosen.

But we chose to do it nonphysically for various reasons. First of all, we did not see the necessity, and did not feel the necessity, of encumbering ourselves in that density. Furthermore, in our particular levels of growth and advancements, we have come to realize that for our own preferences and for our own desires, we could accomplish much more of what we wanted to accomplish nonphysically. We could accomplish the destiny that we have selected by doing so without body form, without prejudicing ourselves, so to speak, by the limitations and by the uniqueness of what it is to be physical.

We can exist, and do exist, for example, outside of the Set of "All Those Who Have Ever Been or Ever Will Be Physical." Thus we can have a grander appreciation and perhaps a grander understanding of the physical, ironically, because of that particular positioning. We made the choice, also, because we knew we could more elegantly fulfill a destiny that, without time, we knew we were already fulfilling (present participle — we use "fulfilling" advisedly). At the point of original choice, our future is already happening and influencing those original choices. We made our choice to be nonphysical.

*Craig Steel, **Together Books**, Denver, Colorado*

Q: Can we look forward to your emanating a physical body at any time for further teachings?

Lazaris: No. Quite clearly, no. We've looked at the consideration and indeed, no. Once upon a time someone asked us whether, if we were very, very good, we would be allowed to have a body. Laughingly we responded that we *are* "very, very good," and we feel that we are quite happy with our decision not to incarnate in physical form. We communciate verbally, one-to-one and in workshops. We communciate by audio and video tape. Most recently we communicate in written form — books. We do not need a body.

Q: Are you saying that to a certain extent it's more facilitative for you to utilize a nonphysical form than a physical body?

Lazaris: Much more! Yes, because we're without prejudice. You who are physical have a prejudice in terms of what it is to be physical. You have attachments, connections, and biases. You have beliefs and attitudes that are hooked into that physicalness and that anchor you in many ways. You have thoughts and feelings that are very, very human, very physical. You make choices and decisions along that same line.

Our perspective is separate from that, and therefore we can be without prejudice. We can be without bias, without the emotional predeterminations that you might otherwise have. Therefore, our observations can be more objective, and more independent, and therefore perhaps more insightful than they would be if we were so encumbered with a body.

L azaris: Certainly so. There are many who have incarnated in body form to be teachers. Their physicalness did encumber them. However, in many ways one might suggest that both Jesus and Buddha were channeling the consciousness that is referred to as the God Consciousness or the Christ Consciousness.

Paul Zuromski, **Body, Mind & Spirit**, Johnston, Rhode Island

Q: The reason I ask this question is because of the obvious examples of Jesus and the Buddha incarnating ...

The Question of "We"

L azaris: "We" is the plurality of ourselves. Certainly not the nobility or the imperialness of us — no, not at all! But rather, as you are aware of yourself as a singular being, you also know, at least intellectually, that you have other aspects of yourself.

You know, for example, that there's a child and an adolescent. You know there's an astral self, and there is a Higher Self, and there are different levels of lifetimes that you've experienced that are truly simultaneous to this lifetime.

Since all time is an illusion, we would suggest, those that are called past lifetimes and future lifetimes are really simply lifetimes that are occuring simultaneously, but in a different time frame than what you experience now.

You know, there are many "you's" and many aspects of who you are. Because you are intellectually aware of those, but only emotionally aware of yourself as singular, you refer to yourself as "I".

In our reality, we are aware of the multiplicities of our own levels, and the existences that we have on

Q: You always refer to yourself as "we."

many different levels of awareness at the same time, both intellectually and emotionally. And therefore, we refer to ourselves in the plural as "we". And that's what the "we" is, so to speak.

Q: Is that why it's so difficult to explain what it is like in realities other than this one?

Lazaris: Absolutely. You have a linear reality that you have created, and you have a linear language to go along with that reality, and therefore to talk outside of time and space, in language alone, is difficult enough. And indeed, to conceptualize outside of time and space, beyond that fourth dimension, is even more difficult.

"What's a day in your life like, Lazaris?" Well, we don't have "days." So therefore, how can we relate to you? "What did you feel like yesterday?" That doesn't make any sense to us at all. Nor does the sentence: "How do you feel today?"

We have to know that that's a colloquialism of your language that means something to you, and it's a positive statement, a friendly statement, and our response to that is supposed to be: "Oh, just fine. Everything is just fine." So we make the verbal responses — not even verbal responses at that — we make the vibrational responses that sound like verbal responses to answer such a question that indeed doesn't even make sense.

So it does become rather difficult to relate to you what our reality is like in that regard! That is so.

Paul Zuromski, **Body, Mind & Spirit,** *Johnston, Rhode Island*

Lazaris: When you grow up, you come to this realization that God is not a man with arms and legs and intestines and a stomach. God is a force. God is an energy. God is love, as it tells you in your New Testament. God is light. Therefore, God is a nonphysical being in that way. And you'll accept that you're physical — we hope there's not too much argument about that! But there's an assumption that there's nothing in between you and God.

We're not saying we're physical, that's true, and we're not saying we're God, either. We are saying that there are realms of reality that exist somewhere between where you are and where that ultimate force — that ultimate energy — lies. Let us say that we lie in the "past-middle" region. We are a light, an energy, a force, an intelligence that exists without body form, without the encumbrance of physicality.

Therefore, we like to see ourselves as a spark, a spark of love, a spark of light, a spark of God. And you and we are both the same. We just know it more clearly than you do.

*Craig Lee, **LA Weekly**, Los Angeles*

Q: How do you define the nature of your existence?

The Realms of Lazaris

Lazaris: Well, certainly. It wouldn't be so much "plane" as a singularity, but "planes" in the plural. Perhaps the easiest way to describe this is to explain that you have what we call "The Lower Worlds" — and lower in this case is simply a position, not an evaluation — that are made up of four planes of reality. One of those planes, of course, is the one you're most aware of (maybe not as familiar with as you'd like, but

Q: Tell us a little bit about your plane of reality. What's it like where you are?

most aware of), and that is the Physical Plane of Reality, which includes not only your Earth, but all the galactic systems, and any other life forms that are "out there" that are of a physical nature. They all belong to this plane of reality that is called the Physical Plane.

Beyond that (and we don't say above it or below it, to left or right, but "beyond it" because all growth is exponential — in all directions simultaneously) is what is referred to most commonly as the Astral Plane of Reality. That is the frequency where everything is a conceptual replication of what is or could be physical.

Beyond that is what we call the Causal Plane of Reality. That's the plane of all cause and effect. It is the plane of all possibility within which is your possibility, within which is the probability and ultimately the actuality of what you will manifest in your physicalness.

Beyond that is the Mental Plane of Reality which, in most religious senses, is heaven. That's where most of the traditional gods and goddesses of religions past, present, and future reside. This is the bliss, the utopia, to which most refer. Biblically, there is a reference to the three heavens, and that there is a third heaven about which no words can be spoken, referring to the Astral and Causal Planes, and then to the third, the Mental Plane.

Those four worlds are the realities that you have created yourselves as human beings, perhaps not with as much conscious awareness as you'd like, but nonetheless you have created those worlds. Beyond those worlds there are many, many planes. They are numbered, perhaps, but they do not have names. On a certain number of these higher planes, that are quite a bit beyond those that you have created, are the planes of reality upon which we exist.

We do not have form. We do not have a body — never have. We do exist as a consciousness, a spark, as we perhaps describe it, a spark of light, a spark of love, a spark of energy, a spark of consciousness. Any of these terms is perhaps quite useful.

We do not think, but rather we create thought. We do not experience externally to ourselves, but we create experience.

"'What plane are we on?' we've been asked. 'Give it a number. We'll be there.'"

We do not have days or nights or time. We exist simultaneously and continuously. Our "days," to put it in your terms, are filled basically with creating thought, creating and experiencing emotion, and generating realities for our own observation, and for our own experience.

We also spend a great deal of "time" — which in our reality we don't have — doing exactly what we're doing upon the Physical Plane: communicating, educating, informing, working to bring understanding and knowledge. About 1% of our energy is devoted to this work upon the Physical Plane. That is not meant to be an insult, just an explanation.

We also work in the same way with many consciousnesses who have long since moved beyond the Physical Plane. We are helping them understand, helping them grow, and giving them a perspective so that they might take back their own power, so that they might explore their own understanding more completely.

Thus our "time" is spent. When you take our experience and put it into linear language and thought, it can sometimes sound a little boring. "All you do is sit around and create thought and create experience and create emotion and feel it?" Yes, and we teach and work and expand and laugh and create joys and create wonderful mystical and marvelous realities to explore. And that's, in a sense, what we do.

"What plane are we on?" we've been asked. "Give it a number. We'll be there."

Actually, numbers would be totally meaningless. Also, growth is not about "well, whose teacher is on what level?" One should measure a teaching by the quality of the work. One should measure by the value of the work. One should measure by the fruits of the labor, as it says in your Bible.

We don't want people listening to us "because Lazaris said so, and he's from such-and-such a plane of reality." We want people to listen because "Hey, what he says makes sense, and more than makes sense, it really works. And more than really works, it has really benefitted me. That's why I want to listen."

That's why we want you to listen.

So we basically say, "What plane would you like us to be on? We'll meet you there."

Mary Pratt & Jack Clarke, New Age Information Network, Atlanta

How Lazaris Learns

Lazaris: Yes. All right. Well, how fascinating, indeed! And your intent here to come up with questions that have not been asked so far has been quite successful, most definitely so!

To the first: Who are our mentors or our teachers? To begin, we might say that as far as names or identities that you of the Physical Plane might relate to, we must respectfully apologize and say that there are none. Indeed, on our own levels, we are primarily our own mentor, our own teacher. The one to whom we refer most frequently in our growth is indeed ourselves.

We refer to ourselves here in the plural primarily because we are aware of ourselves on many different levels. You sense yourself, for example, as a singular physical being. You think that intellectually. You feel that emotionally. Quite so, you refer to yourself in the singular. Because in our reality we are aware of ourselves on many different levels at the same time, we refer to ourselves in the plural.

Because you emotionally and intellectually sense yourself in that singularlity, you tend to reach outside yourself and experience others as though they are separate, as though they are beyond your own sense. In our reality, we experience ourselves on numerous levels both intellectually and emotionally.

We connect to the higher aspects of ourselves, to "future" aspects of ourselves, and to numerous and various aspects of ourselves that are stretching and reaching on the farthest edges of our own reality. These aspects are our mentors, are our teachers.

Q: We thought it would be valuable to learn more about Lazaris and the spiritual path of Lazaris — about your own spiritual path. So our first question is actually three questions:

One: Who are your mentors or teachers?

Two: Could you give us a history of your spiritual path and what obstacles you faced and how you overcame them?

And three: What do you see as your present path for continued evolution of your own consciousness?

We do not need to give them separate identities, separate physical appearances, or separate body forms, primarily because in our reality there is no body form! We don't have a body form, nor does anybody else on our planes, for that matter. So in that regard we can stretch and reach and touch higher and different aspects of ourselves from which to learn, and so in that way we are our own mentor — indeed our own teacher.

There are other consciousnesses, like us, who exist upon the planes of reality we do, and through interaction they have become our teachers as well. In other words, other consciousnesses, like ourselves, aware of themselves in the multiplicity of dimensions, exist on the multi-planes where we exist. We interact with them; we "talk with them." We involve ourselves with them, and through that communication we grow, we stretch, and we explore our spiritual path in a way that is similar to the way you interact with people in your reality. The difference: You are aware of your boundaries, and the differences and the separations between the two of you.

When we interact, we meld those "boundaries." We become one. In that way we can learn perhaps more completely and more thoroughly from such interaction and such communication with others on our own levels. Those are our teachers, our mentors — ourselves and those with whom we interact.

We would add that we are the only one from our levels who is, who ever has, and who ever will be communicating with your Physical Plane. One of the concepts that we teach is Elegance — expending the least amount of energy to gain the maximum benefit. On our levels of reality all things function with elegance, meaning that since we are communicating and interacting with your Physical Plane, there is no need for any other upon our planes of reality to do so.

"Without time there is less than a momentary difference between us and the others on our planes of reality when we interact with you. When you interact with us, you are interacting with them."

Realize something: Without time there is less than a momentary difference between us and the others on our planes of reality when we interact with you. When you interact with us, you are interacting with them. When we interact with you, they are interacting with you.

To the second issue: What has been the history of our spiritual path? It is rather difficult to answer the question in that we do not have time! Therefore, to say something has been or something is or something will be, as somehow distinct from one another, is virtually impossible.

We don't have a history. Our spiritual path has always been and always will be. We suggest it is the same as it always has been. We explore different arenas of our spirituality simultaneously. In fact, a history would be impossible to delineate.

Being aware of your language, and being aware of the linear aspects of your particular world, let us add this: Our spiritual growth "began" with the exploration of emotion. Again, the words make no sense to us, but we are using them hopefully to make some sense to you. Our spiritual growth began with the exploration of emotion, all contracting and expanding emotion. We do not refer to them as negative or positive.

Our "initial" experience of growth was to discover ourselves in each and every emotion that was available, both the contracting and expanding emotions. We have moved beyond those emotions. We have dropped away the contracting ones, so that now we are exploring and experiencing only those which are the expanding emotions. Primarily, you could find all these emotions in the singular word called Love. That has been, in a sense, the "evolution" of our growth.

Beyond that, intellectually we create thought, and therefore we don't think. We don't "think about this" or

"As you will stretch and reach ... as you will move in the direction of what we call the Full Self, or the Realized Self, you will discover the Future Self. Stretch and reach for that Future Self and the Higher Self that lies beyond it. We would encourage you."

"think about that" or grow in our thinking capacity. We create thought. Perhaps a way to describe this, in a way that makes sense to you, is that we began by creating "little thoughts," and we have grown and expanded our own expertise to the point where now we create "very, very big thoughts." That's the second aspect of the evolution.

Thirdly, we have no physicality, you see. Therefore, we haven't grown in a physical way whatsoever.

There are four possible categories — four possible arenas — in which to grow: physically, emotionally, intellectually and finally intuitively.

We have already suggested how we grow emotionally and intellectually. Intuitively, let us say that we have become increasingly aware of the magnitude of our own awareness. Those words seem to be somewhat convoluted, we understand.

Perhaps we can be clearer: We have stretched and reached so that we have become more and more aware of our own capacity to be aware. We have stretched our own realization of God/Goddess/All That Is. We have become increasingly aware that we are, as you, a piece of God/Goddess/All That Is, becoming a bigger piece of God/Goddess/All That Is. That has been our intuitive capacity of growth.

To offer you a bit of direction ... Realize that you have four limited selves. You have a limited self of physicalness, of intelligence, of emotion, and of intuition. As you can allow each of these components of you to become the maximum of what they can be, you will evolve with Elegance.

Physically become as healthy as you possibly can, as healthy as *you* can possibly become — not by comparison to others — but as healthy as *you* can become.

Emotionally, feel the fullest, the richest, and the deepest extent of your own emotions.

Intellectually, allow yourself to think, to think intricately and intimately. Allow yourself to have a richness of thought.

Intuitively, allow yourself to open up to trusting yourself and then to trusting those who are worthy of your trust. Allow yourself to open up to being more intuitive and more in tune with your reality. Allow yourself to open up to having a higher sense of resonance with Nature, a higher sense of what we call Dominion (as opposed to Domination) in your world.

As you will stretch and reach in each of these four capacities, being the most you can possibly be physically, the most you can possibly be emotionally and intellectually, being the most you can possibly be intuitively — as you will move in the direction of what we call the Full Self, or the Realized Self, you will discover the Future Self. Stretch and reach for that Future Self and the Higher Self that lies beyond it. We would encourage you.

Hopefully that has answered your questions....
... We tend to do that. Yes.

... and a few down the list.

Craig Steel, **Together Books**, Denver, Colorado

Q: Lazaris, do you have an unconscious and a Higher Self? Please explain.

Lazaris: All right. We though we'd start off with some simpler questions ... {laughter} ... Do we have an unconscious mind, a subconscious mind, indeed a conscious mind, and how about a Higher Consciousness as well? And the answer is: Yes, yes, yes and yes ... {laughter} ... We do indeed have a Higher Self. We do indeed have a subconscious, an unconscious and a conscious self. The difference is that in our reality we are aware of them. We refer to ourselves in the plural as "we" because of our multi-planes of awareness and because we know and are connected consciously to our subconscious mind and to our unconscious mind. We are our own Higher Self. Yes, we are our own Higher Self.

Because we do not have time in our reality, we are aware of the beginning of reality, the middle, and the end of it simultaneously. It all happens "at once." Therefore, we are at one with, and consciously aware of, our subconscious mind and our unconscious mind. We are our own Higher Self. Yes, we are our own Higher Self.

"We are constantly involved in expanding our awareness. We are constantly involved in the reach and stretch of growth.

"Yes, there is more. There is always more...."

We access these "selves" fully consciously as we communicate with you and with the multitude of consciousnesses with whom we interact. So yes, we have those components.

To add to that, we are also involved in growth. Some people think, "Well, Lazaris, you must be done!" You're never done. No one's ever done. No consciousness ever stops growing. We know that there are certain teachings that suggest that you reach a certain state of bliss. The Judeo-Christian ethic and many of the traditional religions of your planet all speak of a heavenly state where you exist in a state of bliss — where you sit and sing "Hallelujahs."

If you ever really stopped and thought about it for more than about a minute and a half, you'd realize that that doesn't sound too entertaining. ... {laughter} ... Over and over again, "Hallelujah! Hallelujah! Hallelujah!" Yes? Sing the praises. "Praises, praises, praises." Yes? It gets a bit old, yes? There are certain states of awareness that are perhaps much more blissful than others, but whatever level you acquire, there's always more. There is always more ...

We are constantly in a state of growth and in a state of expanding our awareness of ourselves and of our realities. That growth and expansion is happening, however, simultaneously, which is very difficult to say and more difficult to understand because you have a linear language.

When you say, "It happened, and is happening, and will happen, and it's all mooshed together as one," it's difficult to understand. Nonetheless, it is happening that way. We are constantly involved in the reach and stretch of growth.

Yes, there is more. There is always more....

Anonymous Question, Evening with Lazaris, Atlanta, 1987

Q: Will you explain the characteristics of emotion as they are experienced in your dimensions?

Lazaris: We have to use linear language here, so please understand that when we say "there was a time," we are really meaning "there is/was/will be a point of consciousness." So, "there was a time" when the full gamut of emotion from love to hate was part of our experience. We felt all emotions that were contracting and that were expansive.

Now we are in a place and have evolved into the reality where the emotions that we feel are always expansive and expressed, and therefore always positive. We never "don't express" an emotion, and the ones we have are always the celebratory emotions. In other words, we feel love, happiness, laughter, humor, joy and fun. We feel the full range of those celebratory emotions.

Therefore, we don't get angry, and we don't have hurt. We don't get afraid, and we don't have frustration or anxiety. We know those emotions, because there was "a time" when we explored those emotions as well.

Through the exploration we have released many emotions because ultimately there is only the state of love. Therefore, as one grows and grows and grows and realizes and expands, one eventually more closely approaches God/Goddess/All That Is. In that approach, one is inundated only with the celebratory emotions.

" ... there is the total eruption of light, the total eruption of energy, and there is as total as total can be an experience of God/Goddess/All That Is that is all-encompassing."

People sometimes say, "Oh, Lazaris, please don't be angry with me because I didn't do the technique you suggested last time." We never get angry, in that sense.

Sometimes people try to project father onto us. They say, "Oh, I bet you really hate me now." No. No, we never feel those feelings. We make no judgments, in that sense. Those emotions ... One "time" we could, perhaps, have felt them, but we don't have that desire, and therefore we don't do it any longer.

How do we feel emotions? Well, they don't "happen" to us. It's not as though an external force has happened — something out there. There's no "out there" in our reality. It's all "in here," so to speak.

In here what happens when we feel joy, for example, is an eruption of energy that is perhaps an eruption of an awareness of God. When there's happiness, there's an eruption of an awareness of God, and when there is a sense of humor and laughter, there is an awareness of the music of God, because surely the laughter of the spheres and the music of the spheres are the same.

Therefore, it's hard to describe it other than to say that there is the total eruption of light, the total eruption of energy, and there is as total as total can be an experience of God/Goddess/All That Is that is all-encompassing. We feel only the celebratory emotions, because ultimately they are what the energy of God/Goddess/All That Is, is.

Patricia Clay, Infinite Thought, San Diego

Channeling Only through Jach

Lazaris: No, we never have. This is the first time we have done this kind of work with the Physical Plane. We don't have time in our reality, so it's rather difficult to put it into your words, but for as long as you can possibly conceive of time we have been working with consciousnesses as they move through their evolutionay levels and come within our realms.

Presently, we are working with a number of consciousnesses who had their last physical incarnation on the Earth Plane in Lemuria. When they left they realized they need not return to physicality, and thus began their various tasks of moving forward from level to level. They have finally reached our levels, and we work with helping them grow.

We have not communicated with other planetary systems, and other systems of that sort. We have not communciated with your Earth Plane other than in this one particular timing. We have been aware of your Earth,

Q: You have said that you will only channel through Jach. But do you perhaps channel through any other person in another time or on another planet?

and we have watched it as well as other planetary systems. We have been intrigued by your physical evolution, but it is only at this time that we have decided to make our observations more apparent.

We will continue to talk with people for the remainder of the life of the Channel. When he chooses to depart, which is not for a number of years, we similarly will depart.

We've not channeled through anyone else on this planet or any other in the past, nor do we intend to in the future.

We make it very clear to people that we are not here forever. We want you to learn from us, not to become dependent on us.

Paul Zuromski, **Body, Mind & Spirit,** *Johnston, Rhode Island*

Q: Are you working with any other parallel Physical Planes now?

Lazaris: No. Your Earth Plane is the only Physical Plane that we're working with. Again, a major part of our philosophy is the function of Elegance, which, as we describe it, is not a fashion trend, but rather a scientific term that refers to the maximum result with the least amount of energy expended. Therefore, as we examined the Earth's plane, with the decision to so communicate, it was your planet with which we wanted to connect.

One reason is that your planet is tremendously spiritual. You know, there are so many on your planet who rather put themselves down, criticize themselves and blame themselves. As Americans you tend always to think that you're the "bad guys," that somehow you're the culprits in this world.

As a planet you tend to do the same thing, and you think extraterrestrials are all hovering around you because you are such slow, retarded people that you're somehow so far behind the rest of the cosmos.

Many "spiritual teachers" (and we put those words in quotations) tell you that sort of thing — that they're here, the masters, the brothers, the guardians are here because you're so slow. They imply — if not directly state — that you human beings are so far behind that you're somehow impeding the growth of the cosmos.

Clearly that's not the case. Your planet is a radiant ball of light. There's a tremendous amount of spirituality. Many of those who come to observe you are observing you not because you're so far behind, but because in many ways you're so far ahead. They're coming to see what you have, what the secret that you have is that makes you so spiritual, so loving, so seeking of God/Goddess/All That Is.

"Your planet is a radiant ball of light. There's a tremendous amount of spirituality. Many of those who come to observe you are observing you not because you're so far behind, but because in many ways you're so far ahead."

Maybe your technology is not the most advanced. Maybe you can't travel through time and space as some of those other humanoid forms from others systems can, but you can love, and you can forgive, and you can move forward, and you can change. You can seek a God/Goddess/All That Is more beautifully and more consistently than most planetary systems that are out there. Because of that beauty, we are here.

Beyond that, of course, we are here to connect with the one who is Peny because we, in our observations, are rather pleased with her patterns of growth, pleased with her particular goals and want to be of assistance — not to do it for her — but to be of assistance.

Also, observing the Channel in his particular growth patterns, we became very aware that he would be an ideal channel for us. If we're going to communicate we want to make sure what we say, what we send, is actually what comes out, and that it is not interfered with by his prejudices or limitations. So therefore, for these various reasons, we communicate with the Earth and with you on the Physical Plane.

*Mary Pratt & Jack Clarke, **New Age Information Network**, Atlanta*

Q: Everybody who's channeling claims that their spirit entity, whoever it might be, is exclusive with them. We're all part of the same whole ... we're just expressions. How do you deal with a question like that? In other words, if we can access anywhere, how can there be exclusivity?

Lazaris: Oh, certainly so. We say very clearly that we have chosen the particular channel we have chosen, and we are quite pleased with our choice for various reasons, not the least of which is the clarity with which we can so communicate through this particular channel. And therefore, as long as he's about, so we will channel through him exclusively. We will not channel through others in this verbal sense.

At the same time, we tell you, and we mean it very sincerely, that we will Blend, as we call it, Blend with your energies. We will not Blend with you to create your reality *for* you, clearly not. Indeed some have claimed: "Give it to me. I will create your reality for you." One: That's not true. And secondly, it's a tremendous rip-off, using your vernacular, of your power.

We will Blend with you, we will work with you, and we will create *with* you your reality. There are thousands of individuals who, in their meditative processes, have tapped into our energy, have asked us for help or understanding, have asked us for direction, which they have received, but they don't "channel" us. They don't all of a sudden start speaking the words. That will not happen.

We make it very clear: This is the only body through which we will channel, but it is not the only body with which we will make contact, which we will touch. We will touch you if you allow.

Indeed, you do create your own reality, and therefore, if you want to communicate with Lazaris, or you want to communicate with Seth, or you want to communicate with some of Edgar Cayce's energies, one can indeed do that. One can indeed call those energies in, but to turn around and say that you are now channeling Edgar Cayce, or channeling Lazaris, or channeling Seth, no, that would be a separate kind of distinction.

We make the distinction very clear because we want our message to be very clear. And thus, if others claim to be channeling us, it would be difficult to say, "Well, this is what Lazaris says on this point." Well, which Lazaris?

We make it clear. Growth is difficult enough as it is. It need not be made more difficult. Therefore, we make it clear that this communication that is verbal, this communication that is out loud or written, will come only through the particular channel that we have chosen exclusively. Beyond that, your contact, your interaction, your Blending, your meditative relationship with us, that is your own. It is quite personal and private, and indeed it can be very real....

... And we're going to keep using it, yes! Absolutely! Why mess with success?

*Paul Zuromski, **Body, Mind & Spirit**, Johnston, Rhode Island*

"We make it very clear: This is the only body through which we will channel, but it is not the only body with which we will make contact, which we will touch. We will touch you if you allow."

... So what you're saying is that you've found a great communications device ...

Q: You've said that you will be with us only as long as Jach Pursel survives — as long as his body survives. Why is that? Why not longer?

Lazaris: Partly because we are not here to save the planet. We're not here on a mission that is something that has to be done. We are not here in such a way as to say we are a necessity of your planet, but rather we are a preference.

We say very clearly that we will be communicating for as long as the Channel survives so as to imply that we're not somehow an institution, that we're not somehow something that has to be, or something that you must absolutely get involved with. Rather, we are a preference, an energy along the way that you can involve yourself in or not, depending upon your own desire, your own preference. That's the first reason.

The second reason is that we are very particular about the fact that our communication be as clear and as complete and as whole as it is, and therefore we spent, in your Earth time, what would be many hundreds of years, in a certain sense, making the adjustments and the necessary fine tuning points so as to make sure that what you hear is actually what we said.

The clarity of the channel is very important. Therefore, once this particular vehicle is through and the body is no more, we do not want to have to rely upon developing a secondary channel.

Thirdly, far too many in this world of channeling have, in a certain sense, jumped on the bandwagon. It is rather sad to us, for example, that after Jane Roberts chose to leave the planet all of a sudden there must be at least 100 or 150 people who are claiming to "channel" Seth, the "original," the "real one," when Seth had said that he would only communicate through her. It's very sad, because what happens then is the words, the beautiful communications that Seth did put forth, get polluted by people saying, "Well, Seth said this" or "Seth said that." Well, wait a minute. Are you talking about the

Seth of Jane Roberts, or are you talking about one of the myriad of other "Seths" whom a number of people subsequently claimed to "channel?" Most of the other "Seths" contradict the real one. They do not communicate the same clarity, the same information, or the same consistency of information.

After the Channel's body is no longer, we know there suddenly would be some who claimed to be communicating with or channeling "Lazaris." To avoid that, we try to make it as clear and as consistently clear as possible that we will not be channeling through anyone else in any other time or in any other capacity.

Lazaris: Yes, it was premeditated on our part, most definitely so. The term is somewhat strange because premeditation implies time. In your linear linguistics we have to use such words as preparation, premeditation, or predetermined in some capacity, though we would clearly suggest as soon as you move outside of time those terms become totally meaningless.

Q: So using Jach Pursel was premeditated on your part.

Let us put it this way: We knew we wanted to communicate to your Earth planet. We made that decision, that choice. We do create our own reality as well — we do not teach anything that we do not abide by ourselves.

In that decision and choice, in the whole activity of developing the energy around communicating to your planet, and the elegance of such communication, we needed to find a clear channel. As well, we had a desire, very clearly, to deal with the one who is now called Peny.

We wanted to interact with her. We like her vibration. We like what she is about, and realized: She is one human being we would like to establish contact with, to comm
unciate with.

The way we could best connect with her — to touch her — would be to channel through the one who is now called Jach. Knowing that, seeing the future, the past, and the present simultaneously, we began to have impact.

In what would be called your past, hundreds of years ago, we began subtly, ever so subtly, nudging — and we use the word nudging quite advisedly, because we did not control, we did not possess, we did not insist that "he must do this or must do that." We gently nudged, gently made suggestions on the wisp of the wind. The Channel took those various turns through the various progression of simultaneous lifetimes. He allowed himself to be aligned as he entered this current lifetime so that he would be in the best position to allow this connection to occur.

In this current lifetime, we have had certain influences, ever so subtle, admittedly. We have nudged this way, nudged that way, and encouraged an emphasis here and discouraged one there so that when it came time, when the time was right (and that happened in your Earth time of the year 1974), that connection between him and us could be done rather elegantly, without a lot of hassle, without a lot of stress, or a lot of difficulty.

We're quite pleased with the work that we did, for indeed as we began this communication, the clarity was rather there. We are consistently able to communicate with clarity.

Subsequently, we have been able to strengthen that clarity. We've been able to strengthen that energy so as to become even clearer, which has been of great satisfaction to us as well. To that extent, premeditated? Yes. To that extent preplanned.

It was not "ordained" or "destined." Those words are too strong. However, it was planned and organized in such a way that would allow the moments of consciousness to come together in such a way as to create this phenomenon. It happened rather successfully.

David Rogers, Llewellyn's New Times, St. Paul, Minnesota

How Lazaris Experiences

Q: How do you perceive an individual like myself from your perspective?

Lazaris: Well, how we perceive you is perhaps best described this way: If you were to take 100 film projectors with 100 different movies in them, and show them all on one screen, that's in a sense what we perceive. We sense this wonderful maze of color, this wonderful maze of shapes, this wonderful maze of sounds that are you. We sense all your lifetimes that have ever been or ever will be.

We then sort through that vibratory mish-mosh, as it might well be seen, and find that energy, that essence, that is you. From there, we can perceive the essence, the spirit, the piece of God that is in you, the light, the spark that indeed you are.

We look for the beauty of humanity, not the limitation. As we look for the unlimited beauty, we can find it, so we can point it out to you and hope that you can find it in yourself, too. That is a major part of what we do when we work with individuals and with groups of people individually. We perceive you that way.

Paul Zuromski, Body, Mind & Spirit, Johnston, Rhode Island

Q: One of the questions I've always had is: Never having lived here and shared time here, there's so much about Earth, day to day ... I call it Earthism ... day-to-day trivial things that you know about. It's always been a curiosity to me where you learned all the colloquialisms.

Lazaris: Well, we've made a point of learning them, and we have a number of resources: First of all, we can tap into the Channel's memory banks, and therefore we tap into certain of his experiences for purposes of analogy and explanation. Also, we have access to those with whom we speak, although we do not mind read. We purposely stay away from that. There's no point and no value in that at all — but we do tap into your consciousnesses, and, therefore, we will often adapt vocabulary so as to be more accessible. Plus, of course, there is the Collective Unconscious, of which Jung spoke, which also contains all of that input and information.

Additionally, because we are outside the Set of all those things, of "Earthism," as you call it, we can therefore overview and see them quite clearly. We purposely use the vocabulary, the vernacular, and the colloquialisms because our goal here is to be approachable. We use the body to gesture, to inflect our words, and to become very conversational, in that regard, rather than talking perhaps as a computer might talk.

We've worked for the many "years" that we have been communicating to your Earth so that we appear more and more human, so that we appear more and more appoachable. We do not want people feeling as though they're sitting "in audience" with us. We want to be sitting together, having a conversation and interacting. And thus we make a point of being alert to those particular issues and of being able to use the vernaculars as appropriately as possible.

Mary Pratt & Jack Clarke, New Age Information Network, Atlanta

The Accent

Lazaris: In all the years that we have been talking, which has now been almost 14, many people have asked about the accent. One: Why do we even have one since we have never been physical? We don't have a national background from which to draw. We don't have past lifetimes in your world upon which to base a language. And that's very true. Then why have we chosen this particular accent? We rather somewhat tongue in cheek suggest that we don't have an accent. … {laughter} …

Nonetheless this is our explanation, very clearly so: First of all, we don't have a form. Therefore, we don't really talk at all. We don't speak. We don't communicate by words, clearly not, and certainly not in a language.

But we do generate vibration. We do generate vibration, and we have (in your language, "over a period of time") rather observed and learned how to create certain vibrations, that when they are transmitted through the ethers — for lack of a better word — enter into what would be called the Mental Plane of Reality, downstepping to the Causal, the Astral, and ultimately into the Physical Realm.

They are still transmitted simply as vibrations, which by that point, have taken on a certain … how do you say? … electromagnetic quality perhaps that indeed is still being transmitted. They then become … how do you say? … channeled through this body that we are currently using.

The vocal cords create what? Vibrations. And they are like cords (and that's why they're called vocal

Q: Since you create your own reality, I've always wondered how you decided to speak through the Channel with a Scottish-English accent instead of a Nebraskan or New England accent. … {laughter} … How did you decide, and why?

cords) that create a certain vibration that comes out of this particular orifice. That vibration then gets amplified again through the microphone, certainly so. Your ears still have not heard a single word.

As you know from your own understanding of your biology and of your body/brain function, your ears, with their parabolic shape, pick up these vibrations. The vibration is amplified against an eardrum. The eardrum, in turn, transmits that vibration through the ear canal into the brain.

The brain then takes vibration — not words — and turns it into words. You hear not "out here," but inside your head.

Therefore, people have picked up and heard an accent. Some say British; some say Scottish; some say Irish; some say Welsh; some say it sounds French; some say it sounds as though we learned English in India; others say it sounds Oriental. Others say they can't understand a single word we're saying. ... {laughter} ...

It is you who have decided that we have an English and Scottish accent rather than Nebraskan or New England accent. That's part of the answer.

The other part of the answer ... Linguists have rather studied our speech patterns and our sounds. They have discovered that it isn't really any particular accent, but is an amalgamation of many, many, many different accents. That's what the professionals say, and truly so, they are correct.

"It is you who have decided that we have an English and Scottish accent rather than Nebraskan or New England accent."

With the vibrations and their unique sounds, we are putting them in a particular sequence of order that can make sense to you. Also, we put them in a particular order such that certain sounds come out that are easier for you to hear, and easier for you to absorb, so that when you do listen to us speak to you, it's just as approachable as it possibly can be.

A New England accent would perhaps please some of you here, but it would be rather irritating to other people. A broad Midwestern accent or a Southern accent would be appropriately pleasing in certain regions, but would be rather displeasing to others; similarly with a foreign accent.

Therefore, the combination of sounds is the combination that most universally works, in that sense. Some still will find: "I can't understand." And that's all right. Perhaps you're not ready to hear. We are not for everyone.

Anonymous Question, Evening with Lazaris, Philadelphia, 1988

Q: Why do you always refer to Jach as "The Channel" instead of using his name? Is it to make the distinction between you and Jach even clearer?

Lazaris: Well, there is a very, very esoteric reason for that, you know. And that is because ... In our reality we do not really talk. We don't really have any form. We don't have, therefore, a mouth and vocal cords and all those sorts of things that you, as physical beings, have. And so we don't really talk.

What we rather do is align vibration in a particular order and a particular sequence, and then we transmit those vibrations, and they travel through the various levels of the ethers, or the cosmic realms, as they might be called.

Then they enter into your physical world and therefore are amplified through this throat and come out of this mouth, and in this case are amplified through this microphone, and are coming out of the speakers.

It still is not really words. It is still only vibrations that then your ears, in their particular function, pick up.

And in your brain is where it becomes words. And in your brain is where it sounds as though we are talking in a language that you call English or American or whatever. There are certain sounds that are rather difficult to replicate.

One of those sounds is the soft "a". That's why we talk in that way of saying "rahther" rather than the other word that would be more "raaather". That particular "a" sound is rather difficult and awkward for us to make.

Then when you combine that with the "j" sound, the name Jach, in that sense, is one that is very difficult for us to say ... wouldn't you know. ... {laughter} ...

It's much easier just to call him "The Channel" because the long sound of "a" and the "ah" sound of "a" are much easier vibrations for us to piece together and transmit. Simply because it's difficult to pronounce, we rather avoid the name for the most part.

Anonymous Question, Evening with Lazaris, Atlanta, 1988

I've Always Wondered ...

Lazaris: Yes, yes, he does when we want to use his eyes, when we want to look at the watch and see, "Oh, my goodness, look at that. It's already 10:30 p.m., and we've just barely begun." Yes, we can look at his watch.

Q: With respect, I ask, does Jach ever open his physical eyes while you are channeling through him? If not, why not?

We usually choose not to use his eyes because we don't want to be bothered with the clutter, quite honestly. Not that you're clutter, but we suggest the "illusion" is clutter, and therefore we would rather see you in your purer essence.

We don't see you as flesh and blood. We see you as light and sound and as energy and vibration. That's a much clearer picture for us to look at. We don't want to encumber it with input through these particular sensors called eyes.

Also, with these eyes closed, there's less chance for you to worship us. See, we don't want your worship. We don't want you being followers. People who talk with us or who come to workshops for any length of time don't consider themselves followers.

Sometimes when people show up for the first time they think, "Look at all these followers." On first encounter, some fear they are expected to become followers or devotees. After a short while they know better. When there is no place to sign up and no one signing them up, they realize.

No, they're not followers. They are friends, and our relationships work in that capacity. They're very independent.

With these eyes closed it's harder to worship us. It's harder to feel that sense of worshipping. That's why there are no trappings. There are no special clothes the Channel wears. He wears anything from jeans and a shirt that's untucked to dress pants, a shirt and a tie. He wears everything from very nice clothes to very sloppy clothes. There is no costume or uniform.

There are no rings. There are no relics. There are no little trinkets and things like that that are "Lazaris-isms" ... or whatever. We don't want to give you even that temptation.

Additionally, we could move the body around the stage. We could walk the body around the grounds. But, you see, we have this thing about elegance. We tend to practice what we talk to you about, and we suggest expending the least amount of energy for the maximum amount of result.

By channeling through this body we can touch you there in the back row. Why then should we bother moving it all the way through the crowd? Why should we go back there and touch you when we can do that without having to move the body at all?

The elegance of it is very clear. We could move this body around. It could climb up out of this chair and cross the room and do whatever. If we can move the arms in this capacity, if we can make the face make expressions, certainly so, we can move the rest of the body as well.

Similarly, the Channel has no knowledge of what's being talked about, quite on purpose. At first it was far too frightening to him. He didn't want to know! "Just let me out of here!" ... {laughter} ...

Furthermore, initially the majority of our work was with you individually, over the phone or in person. We talk to you privately. Because there are so many of you, we do more workshops and work with you individually in workshops, absolutely, but when we do work

"That's why there are no trappings. There are no special clothes the Channel wears. ... He wears everything from very nice clothes to very sloppy clothes. There is no costume or uniform.

"There are no rings. There are no relics. There are no little trinkets and things like that that are 'Lazaris-isms'..."

privately with people, they don't want the Channel to know what is being said, and he (the Channel) doesn't want to know what's going on.

People talk to us about very intimate and private issues. It would be very difficult for them to think the Channel's going to know all that. Some people still ask for reassurance of confidentiality, and we offer it to them. Absolutely.

It is possible for him to be consciously aware. It is possible for him to hear. We could pipe it in — flip the switch so that the speakers go on wherever he is, off in his state of floating somnambulism. He could come out of trance being aware of every word that was said, for that particular matter.

We just don't choose to do that, nor does he particularly choose to do it, and that's the way it is. It's not out of the realm of possibility that he could be aware and therefore "conscious" of what's being said.

We just want to be as clear as we can, and we don't care for his editorials, quite clearly ... {laughter} ... so we'd just as soon he went to sleep and let us handle this. And since he is not particularly comfortable in front of crowds of people, he'd just as soon he went to sleep as well! ... {laughter} ...

Therefore, we have him stay in an unconscious state, although that doesn't have to happen. We keep his eyes closed, though that doesn't have to happen, either. We use the sedentary body because at this point in time there's just no need to go wandering around the room, in that particular sense. If we want to touch you, we can touch you, and you can feel that touch as really, as solidly — perhaps even more so — than if this fleshly body were doing the touching. That's why we operate it in this way.

Anonymous Question, Evening with Lazaris, Seattle, 1987

Q: Can you move around? Are you inside the body of Jach when you communicate?

Lazaris: Literally, we are not in this body any more than Dan Rather is inside your television set. ... {laughter} ... We transmit energy, and that energy is down-stepped, as we explain, and is amplified through this body system. The gestures that take place, and the facial expressions that take place, are an outplay of what might be called electromagnetic energy that is amplified and then reamplified so that you can see it and hear it.

So we're literally not in the body. We know at one time in your history of mediumship and trance work, the consciousness of the entity entered the body. We suggest that's a bit archaic and certainly not necessary. We don't make actual entry into the body, but we transmit through the body so that we can touch, so that we can work with you.

We can touch you without necessarily having to move this body about. Indeed in Blendings, as those of you who have experienced them can attest, you can feel us, feel the touch and the energy right there.

Anonymous Question, Evening with Lazaris, Atlanta, 1987

Why So Many Channels?

Q: Why are you and many other channeled entities appearing at this time?

Lazaris: The reasons are numerous. First because you have invited us. What we mean is that you as a consciousness individually and, indeed, collectively as a humanity, nationally and internationally, have basically said, "We are ready to grow. We are ready to reach and to stetch. We want to understand ourselves and our reality more completely and more fully, and we welcome, indeed we invite, the opportunity to learn, the opportunity to stretch, the opportunity to become more of who we are."

That invitation, spoken unconsciously, subconsciously, and indeed by many very consciously, is the invitation that at this time has been put forth. Many are now coming forth to impart, to give knowledge, to help you understand yourself and your world more completely.

Secondly, we would suggest that you have put yourselves, as a world community, into a corner whereby the traditional solutions simply won't work. The traditional, linear solutions to problems that have been readily available and rather nonchalantly applied no longer work. More and more you are confronted with what we call a Rubik's Cube reality. More and more you are confronted with a solutionless world where indeed every solution seems to produce five or six more problems.

Even though you're off there rather nicely protected on your own island (Australia), you nonetheless are still part of a world community, and you realize that what happens in Africa and what happens in South America affects you, directly and indirectly. What happens among what are called the Superpowers affects you on a regular and daily basis.

The problems have gotten to a point that there seem to be no more solutions. Therefore, in that sense, we are here not to give you the solutions on a silver platter, clearly not, but to teach you, to teach you how to find those solutions, to teach you the changes that you need to make in your own consciousness in order to allow new solutions to become evident.

We're here in our own specific energy very much to teach people how to transmute negative energy into positive energy, how to transform negative situations into positive situations, and indeed how to transcend the problems in a reality where there seem to be no

"We're here in our own specific energy very much to teach people how to transmute negative energy into positive energy, how to transform negative situations into positive situations, and indeed how to transcend the problems in a reality where there seem to be no solutions."

solutions. We are here to show you there is a new world and to show you how to create it for yourself.

Thirdly, we are here because you are seeking answers spiritually that your traditional methods of spirituality no longer can supply. We are not putting those traditions down, clearly not, for they have their proper place. They have their proper perspective, and they provided answers for as long as they could.

However, now it is time to expand your awareness, to expand your consciousness, to expand the horizons of your understanding. To do that you seek spiritual answers, you seek a deeper sense of your own spirituality. We respond in order to offer that opportunity for you to complete your own growth.

*Brian Williams, **Unicorn**, Brisbane, Australia*

Why Now?

Q: What prompted you to experience the Earth plane in this manner?

Lazaris: Many assume the answers, and assume that we are here, for example, to save the planet — which clearly we are not. Secondly, some assume that we are here, then, to save humanity — which clearly we are not. We are not here to save either the planet or humanity, because we have enough confidence and enough respect for the consciousness that is here to know that you can be responsible, and you can "save yourselves," if indeed you need saving at all. The planet can well take care of itself, if you and the planet will work together.

We know that there are many who claim to be coming for the purpose of "saving planetary systems" and "saving humanities." We would suggest here that as they grow, perhaps, in their own evolution, they will come to realize and understand that you as human beings are quite capable, quite evolved and quite beautifully evolving so as to be able to handle those concerns yourselves.

The purpose of our "visiting," the reason for our coming to this planetary system that you call Earth, comes down to four particular concerns:

The first of those components has to do with the fact that we are here to help you realize that you do create your own reality. Now that is a concept that has been presented throughout most of your metaphysical history.

Even in that which is called the "Old Age," in comparison with that which has been called the "New Age," it has been a philosophy, a point of view. And it has been aborted this way or that way, or adapted this way or that way, to serve particular and personal needs and purposes from time to time.

But the bottom-line truth is that you do create your own reality. There is no asterisk — there is no fine print. That's it. You do create your own reality. We are here not only to help you understand that intellectually, but also to help you begin experiencing it, and to help you begin working with it, and to help you begin functioning with the power of this truth. We are here to help you live your reality from the perspective of "I create it all — I create it all consciously."

The second thing that we have decided to do in coming and visiting is basically to offer to you and to remind you of — or to help you remember for the first time — the fact that there is choice. There is choice in this particular reality. You do not have to grow through pain. You do not have to grow through the suffering, through the self-denial, and through the struggle which have so often been put forth in what is called the Old Age.

Now admittedly, the teachings of the ancients, and the teachings of the Eastern and the Western Mystery Schools have strongly advocated the necessity of "grand patience," the necessity of enduring great pain, the necessity of struggling, suffering, and going through the pain of self-sacrifice. Struggle has been nobilized. It has been elevated to a position and posture of grandeur.

"But now (and everybody is talking of it) is a New Age — a New Age — which doesn't mean taking the old teachings and re-dressing them and putting new costumes on them and presenting the old ideas all over again."

We clearly suggest: We would not argue with such teachings as the method of the Old Age, the way things used to be done. But now (and everybody is talking of it) is a New Age — a New Age — which doesn't mean taking the old teachings and re-dressing them and putting new costumes on them and presenting the old ideas all over again.

New means new. New means something that hasn't been done before. New means something that has never been experienced, and, therefore, the New Age is perhaps newer than a lot of people want to believe, newer than a lot of people are willing to believe!

Therefore, there is a new way of growing that involves love, light, laughter, and the celebration of life rather than the pain, struggle and anxiety of life. What we are here for is not to force people, by any means, but clearly to offer you a choice: Look, if you want to grow by pain and by struggling, you can do so. We have great compassion for you. We will love you enough to let you do that as well.

But at least let us point out to you, at least let us offer you the choice, that there are other ways. If you'd like to grow through the laughter of life, the joy of life, the love and light of life, through the celebration of life, we want to offer you a way to do that — not only to tell you that it's available, but also to show you how to create it that way.

Thirdly, we are here to remind you of, or to help you remember, your "future." Your world seems very frightening now. It seems so devastating out there. More than ever it feels like wherever you turn, to whomever you talk, you are receiving the message that the world is becoming more miserable and terrible — that it is hopeless. With broken hope and breached confidence, you concluded: "I must have done something horribly wrong."

We are here to remind you that you are loved. You are loved. There is a God, whom we refer to as God/Goddess/All That Is, who does love you, who does care about you, who is concerned with you and your particular growth.

We are here to let you know that, to show you ... not just: "Isn't that wonderful! Wouldn't that be grand! Oh, I wish that were true!" We are here to show you that it *is* true, and to show you the ways you can communicate with that God/Goddess/All That Is, the ways you can be touched such as to have your life so changed and so benefitted by that love that you can say, "I know I'm loved because my life reflects it." That is the statement we want you to be able to make. We want you to know that you are loved.

We also want to help you realize that you do love "good enough." We want to help you begin the Journey Home by recognizing that you *are loved* and that you *can love.*

Finally, the fourth component of why we're here is to open you up to what we call The Dream, to remind you and to teach you that you must dream, that you need to be Dreamers. You need to stretch and reach in your imaginations. You need to have desire and not to put

"New means new. New means something that hasn't been done before. New means something that has never been experienced, and, therefore, the New Age is perhaps newer than a lot of people want to believe, newer than a lot of people are willing to believe!"

"Those solutions lie in your dreams, and therefore let yourself stretch, let yourself reach. Let yourself open your heart and open your mind — not just your heart — open your heart and your mind to the reality: As you dream, as you imagine, as you desire, and as you expect, solutions can come to you."

your desires aside for the betterment of others, but to hold on to your desires for that betterment. You need to have the sense of expectancy, to start really expecting things to work wonderfully with desire and imagination.

We suggest that there are solutions to the problems of your world/reality. To any problem you might conjure, there is a solution. But those solutions lie in your dreams. Those solutions lie in your dreams, and therefore let yourself stretch, let yourself reach. Let yourself open your heart and open your mind — not just your heart — open your heart and your mind to the reality: As you dream, as you imagine, as you desire, and as you expect, solutions can come to you.

In fact, the greatest solutions in science have always come from the dream state. Einstein did not come up with the Theory of Relativity in his laboratory. He first came up with it in his dreams, in a sleep dream, as a matter of fact. In a literal dream of the night, he dreamt that solution and then went into his laboratory to bring it from the dream state into the "real" state, and thus came up with the experimentations that ultimately led to his Theories of Relativity.

All solutions lie initially in the dreams, but you have forgotten to dream, because you are frightened of the problems. Therefore, if you can remember your dreaming, and open your hearts and your minds, indeed the solutions can be found.

Life truly can be the celebratory experience it was always intended to be. This is why we're here. This is the message we want to bring to you.

*Patricia Clay, **Infinite Thought**, San Diego*

Lazaris: There are a number of reasons we have made the decision to become "more public," as you say. The first reason is that back on November 30th and December 1st, 1985, there was a subtle shift in the Earth's vibration. That shift meant that people as a whole would begin to grow more rapidly. Those who had already been involved in metaphysics and spirituality would find their particular growth beginning to accelerate at a rate that would even surprise many of them.

Q: You have been very low-key for many years. Many of us could only find you by word of mouth. In December, 1985, you decided to become more visible through video tapes and your appearance on the Merv Griffin Show. Why did you decide to come out of the cosmic closet, so to speak?

Also, people not really involved in the area of spiritual expansion, but perhaps having toyed with a self-improvement course or a how-to-win-friends-and-influence-people seminar, would find themselves reaching and stretching into a deeper sense of themselves. They would begin looking inward for a core of being which would ultimately lead them on a spiritual journey.

Even those who had made no forays whatsoever in this particular direction would suddenly find themselves interested. They might be drawn to a book or an experience that would introduce them to some very rudimentary, but nonetheless critical, points of spiritual expansion. People were saying, "We want more," so we are responding to that request.

We also wanted to open up an avenue of communication regarding the changing vibration of the Earth. We wanted to offer you help in dealing with the critical state of your world. You who chose to be physical during the latter part of this century will experience life changing more and more rapidly. The future will hang in the balance, as it were. A major part of the reason we have become more visible is to offer choices and alternative ways of looking at the world.

The Earth's energy change has also allowed us to express more deeply and completely what it is we want to say. Therefore, as the door opened, we took advantage of the opportunity to move through to the other side and come out more openly.

Over the years many people have asked us to become more open and accessible. We have gracefully and respectfully declined because it was not the appropriate time. Now the timing, in terms of the Earth and the energies of the Cosmos, so to speak, is right.

There is so much going on out there in the spiritual/ metaphysical movement which unfortunately has become self-serving for some individuals and filled with scare tactics and manipulation for others. We felt compelled to offer an alternative, another way of looking at growth rather than the usual limited scope that so many tend to offer. Therefore, we decided to become more accessible to you.

Paul Zuromski, **Body, Mind & Spirit,** *Johnston, Rhode Island*

The Difference

Lazaris: What we are here to accomplish is friendship. We know that this is rather scary for many people. They would much rather that we were here to be a guru or a master or some sort of power-taking authority, because they're used to that, because they're familiar with that, because they know how to deal with that, either positively or negatively.

Friendship often scares people. You wonder, in that sense, "What have I got that you want to be friends with?" That is quite often the largest and indeed the saddest of the fears that you have as human beings.

Basically, we're here to be friends, to establish a relationship, to establish a connection, to establish a way that we might interact with you to learn of your experience, to learn of your physicality, and we're here so that you might interact with us to learn of us, of our realities, and perhaps learn more clearly and more concisely about yourselves.

We're not here to save anyone, we also say. We're not here to save your planet. We're not here because you're the scourge of the Earth or you're the scum of the universe, but rather, in that sense, because of the beauty and the magnificence of who you are.

We are here perhaps to open a door to give you a mirror to help you see more clearly, indeed, who you really are in the larger cosmic picture of things. We are here because we love you.

We love you as humanity. Yes. We also love you as the individual that you are. Yes.

Yes!

Q: You've made it very clear in your teachings that you have no intention of being anybody's guru or master or father figure. And so what is it that you're really here to accomplish that you're not interested in plugging into those pictures?

*Van Ault, **Magical Blend**, San Francisco*

Q: Would you like to expand on the difference between yourself and other channels? I know that you recommend profound techniques and tools. Do you profess a different style of growth?

Lazaris: In certain ways we are grandly different. In others, we are not much different at all. There are many very powerful and beautiful consciousnesses who are now starting to be channeled through. In the mid-Seventies, when we first began our communication, we were asked if we were going to be "the one." "We will be the only one like us, but no, no, no," we answered, "there will be a grassroots movement all over the country. Not just in California or on the East Coast or wherever, but all over the country those individuals will be emerging who will channel information."

Indeed, the grassroots movement we talked about is happening today. The information varies in degree of significance and importance. Each person seeking such communication will find "the" channel or entity that is right for them — much in the same way as in a traditional religious search people find the form of spirituality that best suits them at the time.

We tend to demystify spirituality. We tend to bring the mysteries that have so long been held in secret out into the open and make them available to everyone. At one time it was very much felt, with the various mysteries and teachings, that only the elite were sophisticated enough to comprehend or cope with that secret data. Unfortunately, many people still go to great lengths and hardships trying to keep hidden these supposed secrets when, in fact, they are not so much secrets as they are truths for everyone. Our work is to bring light to that which has been held in secret … in darkness.

Also, there are many who teach because there are many things to be taught: how to love yourself, how to be more trusting, how to be more open, more vulnerable, more intimate — how to discover the joy in relationships, how to grow this way and that way. Many admonish, and many lovingly instruct: "This is what needs to be done." Few teach you how to do it, and that is where the problem arises. You already know you need to love yourself more — it doesn't take a great amount of wisdom or spiritual insight to come to that conclusion — but you don't know *how* specifically to do that.

Many spiritual teachers and channels just brush aside your confusion by saying, "Do it whatever way you can and however is best for you. I am not here to tell you how to do it. I'm just here to tell you what to do!"

We are different. If you want to love yourself more, we will show you the methods and specific steps to do so. If you want to trust yourself more and develop a greater sense of self-worth, we will teach you the various procedures that not only might work, but also *will* work if you let them.

Similarly, we sense ourselves as different than some entities who tend to look at you as though you were the low-life of the universe. They put forth an energy that implies that physical beings are so far behind that the whole cosmos is somehow waiting for you. It is simply not that way at all. You are very beautiful and powerful beings. You are as much of God as any part of the cosmos. You are not on a lower rung or in a "lesser-than" position.

We respect your decision to grow physically. We respect your methods and means of growth and want to assist you. We wish to show you ways to do what you want to do more elegantly, more effectively and productively.

There are those who have asked how we can know so much about being physical when we have never been physical. We have no attachment or vested interest in it. We did not experience physicality and have no sense that the way we did it was the right way or the wrong way — we simply never did it.

Furthermore, because everything is simultaneous, all time is instantaneous, and all space is now, we have access to observing physical reality in a way that perhaps gives us an objectivity that those who have been physical don't have. We see your reality from a perspective that many times has proved to be more helpful, thus adding to the richness of your experience.

Further, we are different than many because we offer technique. Succinctly, we offer technique that is concise, precise, and that works. If you will allow, we offer techniques that work!

*Paul Zuromski, **Body, Mind & Spirit**, Johnston, Rhode Island*

Q: Lazaris, will you Blend with us even when we are not in a workshop? And what can we do to bring this about?

Lazaris: Yes, we will. Blending is a time that we come into your vibration, but you have to let us in, because we will never intrude. We will never intrude! We will never force ourselves upon you. We'll never show up in your dreams unless you ask us to. We'll never come up into your meditations unless you permit it. We'll never come to you unless you call, because we respect you, because we love you.

Certainly we'll blend with you. Many people have had that experience, where they've gone into a Blending and have known — have experienced — that we were truly there. We were with them.

Indeed, Judy — who gets embarrased every time we talk about her by name because she has this thing about visibility — was in her automobile. She was slipping and sliding down a muddy road, and she was heading right for a tree. She had no options. She very quickly, very spontaneously — very loudly in a screaming call — Blended.

She allowed our help in so that she created the reality — we didn't create it, she did — of stopping but inches from hitting the tree. She knows she did it. She knows we helped her.

Other people have allowed our Blendings in for whatever purposes, absolutely. You see, in that sense some people have said, "Gee, why does it cost so much to be spiritual?" We suggest it doesn't cost anything. It doesn't cost anything. "Well, it costs a lot of money to come to workshops." It costs some money, certainly so, because we want to make sure that it's not just a circus. If you have to pay a certain amount of money, you're going to think twice before you just ... "Well, let's just check this out, Martha! ... {laughter} ... Let's just go see what this is all about." You're going to say, "Hey, I'm not sure I want to be just a curiosity seeker and pay money." It's never too much that you can't afford it, but it is enough that you have to think about it.

We always respect you. We always give you more than you pay for. Therefore, you always get back more than you pay, in that regard. ... {applause} ...

But if you can't come to a workshop for various reasons, there are video tapes and there are audio tapes. "Well, I can't afford $59.95!" It costs three dollars, perhaps five dollars, in your local bookstores to go to a showing.

Blendings are free. All you have to do is to be willing. Be willing.

Some people like to re-create the experience of a workshop they attended. Other people love to play the music "Prelude to Lazaris" and "Lazaris Remembers Lemuria." Some people like to, but that's not necessary.

You don't even have to have a tape. All you have to do is close your eyes and be willing, and you can get all the love, all the caring, all the help you need. You will receive all the help you're willing to have.

We won't do it for you, because that robs you of your power, and we're not in the business of taking your power.

We're not in the business at all.

We're in the joy of being your friend as you grow.

Anonymous Question, Evening with Lazaris, Seattle, 1987

Q: How many more years will you be communicating through Jach?

Lazaris: Lots of them. The Channel determined when he was a child that he was going to live to be very, very old.

Paul Zuromski, Body, Mind & Spirit, Johnston, Rhode Island

With love and peace ...

Lazaris

The Journey of Mysteries

Magick & Wicca — Kundalini — Power Centers — UFOs
Crystals — Brain & Consciousness — Meditation
Harmonic Convergence — Atlantis & Lemuria

Magick & Wicca

Q: What part do you see things like witchcraft, ritual magick, and wicca playing in the coming years as part of this New Age?

Lazaris: Many of the concepts of ceremonial magick and traditional magick — magick with a "k" as it is appropriately spelled (to separate it from the Amazing Randy sort of magic) — and the various forms of witchcraft and Druidic study have, unfortunately, had bad press. Many people, sadly even people within metaphysics, think that such people as witches, magicians, and Druidic priests somehow represent the evil and dark side of things.

It is very sad. In the future, as people continue opening their minds and their consciousnesses, many times they will tap into a part of themselves that at one time was involved in such activities. Therefore, then they will open their hearts, allowing further understanding and appreciation.

Magick, witchcraft, Druidic studies, and other forms of occult activity — as they allow themselves to come more into the light, gently, slowly, not forcing themselves, but gently and slowly coming into the light — will indeed be more and more accepted. They will not necessarily be accepted "instead of," but accepted "also as."

This does not mean that people would give up their more traditional approaches to spirituality, but may encompass or expand to incorporate certain understandings of wicca, certain understandings of magick, and certain understandings of the Druidic studies. Despite the uninformed fear of the consensus reality, these activities have historically been very positive and an integral part of an evolving spiritual movement.

In World War II millions of Jews and Russians were exterminated. That holocaust of life had no justification. Throughout history there have been the witches who have experienced the same sort of humiliation, the same sort of degradation, the same sort of pain, the same sort of destruction. Without the outcry of human compassion that accompanied the holocausts of World War II, they have held strong. They persisted and prevailed. The witches, the magicians and others of these cultures provide a backbone of all spirituality.

Metaphysics has been popular and has been unpopular throughout history. It comes and goes in waves of energy. In the early 1900s you are aware of all of the mediums, the seances, the ectoplasmic manifestations, the trumpets, and all the trappings of spiritualism that were "the rage." It died away and went away.

Then there was the upsurgence of what we call the "*National Enquirer* Psychics," who would come out with their annual and bi-annual predictions. Their popularity would surge and then fall away.

Now there is a tremendous movement of spirituality which we suggest is *not* going to fall away. Much to the chagrin, we're sure, of certain Fundamentalists, we suggest that a New Spirituality is finally born.

But throughout it all, throughout all of history, in favorable times and in unfavorable times, there have been the witches, and there have been the magicians who have, in their private way, in their very special way, in their very personal and loving way, kept metaphysics and spirituality alive. They have kept the candle burning, kept the light in the window. A great deal is owed to them, and a great deal of honor and appreciation is due to those who are truly of the tradition.

Admittedly there are the fringe groups. There are those, similarly, who hop on the bandwagon — the

> "... throughout all of history, in favorable times and in unfavorable times there have been the witches and there have been the magicians who have ... kept metaphysics and spirituality alive. They have kept the candle burning, kept the light in the window. A great deal ... of honor and appreciation is due to those who are truly of the tradition."

beasts that come along with the beauty, we would suppose.

The true tradition is something to be honored and valued, and it will come more into the light, and people will realize, "Oh, is that what you mean by witchcraft? I thought it was old women with cackling voices and warts upon their noses. I thought it was princes into frogs and vice versa. I thought you meant evil black magic."

When people see the truth and the beauty, there will be more of a gentle embracing and gentle accepting. Witchcraft has never asked for anything more. Nor has the magician asked for anything more. Both have simply asked to be allowed to co-exist in a reality. And such co-existence will be more and more allowed over the next many years.

David Rogers, Llewellyn's New Times, St. Paul, Minnesota

Kundalini

Q: Can you explain the term *kundalini* energy, and how we can balance this energy in our bodies?

Lazaris: All right. Well, indeed, the word *kundalini*, of course, is an Eastern concept which represents the coiled serpent, which represents the energy that resides within the *chakra* centers. The story, the myth, and indeed the validity behind it, is that there is this serpent, this energy, this power, this vitality, this electricity, as it has been described in numerous different analogies, that lies deep within you. It lies sleeping, coiled and sleeping, deep within you in what is called the first *chakra*, which is symbolically located at the tail bone, at the coccygeal, at the base of the spine. In the process of enlightenment, you are to awaken the serpent, you are to awaken the serpent and to allow it to uncoil, to stretch its energy. You are to allow it to be potent, to be powerful, and to be fully alive within you. Most Eastern thought is devoted, and indeed many years of one's life are devoted, to the gradual — the very gentle and gradual — uncoiling of this energy.

It has been suggested — and correctly suggested in certain places — that an unwarranted and rather frivolous unfolding of this energy could cause backlash, could cause side effects that could be potentially damaging, at least temporarily, if not permanently. The fear of backlash, the fear of problems, has been over-exaggerated. As one approaches the *kundalini* — approaches the serpent within — and works at developing and opening the *chakra* centers in order, it can be totally safe.

Start with the first *chakra*. That is the center of security, physical security. Begin dealing with your physical security by looking at: "What are my concerns? What are my payoffs? What are my blockages around this issue of security? Why am I afraid of losing my security? What can I do in my process, in my growth, in my education of spiritual awareness so as to assuage my fears, my doubts, and my uncertainties, so as to bolster, so as to balance this first center of physical security?"

Then move to the second center, the *chakra* of the genital area, which refers to pleasure. It refers not just to sexual pleasure, but certainly it is inclusive of that. All pleasures, however, are included in this center. "What can I do? What is my guilt? What's my fear? What are my beliefs about and around this issue of pleasure?" As you can come to understand and to consciously accept or reject those particular beliefs, you can mold and change them so you have a sense of power from that second center.

"In the process of enlightenment you are to awaken the serpent, you are to awaken the serpent and to allow it to uncoil, to stretch its energy. You are to allow it to be potent, to be powerful, and to be fully alive within you."

Then move your energy to the third, the fourth and the fifth *chakras*. The third *chakra* is the solar plexus, dealing with emotions as they relate to you and your world and those around you. The fourth *chakra* represents the heart, and thus deals with self-love, and a love of a deeper, more significant or intimate nature with yourself and with others. The fifth *chakra* deals with expression, clearly so, and therefore relates to the throat and its openness.

The sixth *chakra* deals with the intuitive nature and is located in the forehead, and the seventh deals with the spiritual nature and is located within the center of the brain — for meditative purposes at least.

To work with the *chakras*, work each of these centers individually and collectively. That is the secret. If you deal with the *chakras* one at a time, and only work with one and then leave it behind to move to the next one, then you may cause some repercussions in your raising or awakening of the *kundalini*. However, it will work well to open the first, and while you are opening the first (when you feel a certain confidence), move to the second, keeping the first and now the second operating. Then move to the third, so that you're working with the first, second and third. This conjures up in one's mind the adventure of spinning plates, keeping the first, second and third going simultaneously.

By the time you spin the seventh plate and get it really spinning, you've got to run back to the first, the second, and move up to the third, etc. Therefore, the idea is not to do one and then the next, but rather to do one and then expansively add the other, and add a third, and then add a fourth all the way up into the sixth, and finally open the seventh. More correctly, allow — allow — allow the seventh to open.

Then we should suggest the speed of such opening is really up to you. If you approach it on this basis, you almost could never go "too fast" for yourself. This is the way to take mastery of your own *kundalini* energy. You do not have to require or to depend upon someone else telling you when you're ready to be making those movements. When you open your *chakras* to gain power, it's a shame to turn around and give it away!

*Jim Faubel, **Transformation Times**, Beaver Creek, Oregon*

Power Centers

L azaris: Oh, very much so, yes. The energy vortexes — meaning the circles of energy that are two or three hundred miles in diameter — are located on what are called ley lines.

Q: We have discovered on our property what we feel is an energy vortex. It's a small area of about 13 feet in diameter, but the energy feels very different.

To digress, in your body you have acupuncture points — energy vortexes — that follow along certain meridians or ley lines. Where these meridians are particularly "hot" — where there's an energy point — that's where a needle is applied, electronically or otherwise, or pressure is applied if you're doing acupressure. Simply put, following the meridian to an energy vortex and applying pressure is what produces healing.

Your Earth, as a consciousness, similarly has these "meridians." They aren't so clearly defined as perhaps is the "liver meridian" or the "lung meridian," but they are meridians that flow across the Earth, nonetheless. Where they intersect many times there is an energy point, certainly so, and there will be a power point.

Lazaris: Oh, yes.

Q: Are there a lot of these "mini" power centers?

Some are energy vortexes, and some are "mini" power centers. If one looks more clearly, say, in England, you can follow the line from one point to another.

The ancients and the not-so-ancients built temples, churches, and cathedrals right on these particular power points. Stonehenge and Avebury are two examples. Other standing stone places are similarly located (ironically and coincidentally!) right on those points.

Well, certainly so, England is not somehow privileged to have all these energy patterns and no one else does. Certainly so, your country has them. As one looks at the American Indian cultures, the mound Indians of the Midwest built their mounds along these ley lines. The Western Indians built their *kivas* and other power points and sacred places along these lines as well.

Though they may not have had the vocabulary to call them energy points, meridians, or ley lines, indeed they knew their power. So as you find a ley line — an energy point — on your own property, well, within a certain radius you can definitely feel the energy difference. We would trust it. We would go with it, and we would indeed use that energy to profoundly create and more particularly to create the reality as you desire it. Absolutely. That's wonderful.

Q: We were wondering if we can create a power center on the Earth?

Lazaris: Certainly so. One has to go about it with a certain intentionality: "I'm going to lay out a particular power point." We would encourage you to pick a beautiful point — by your definition — it doesn't necessarily have to be beautiful by everybody else's definition. You can imbue it with power.

How do you do this? It's as simple as it sounds — almost so simple that people would think, "Ah, it can't be true."

Basically, you sit there and love the Earth. We recommend that you sit with bare feet to touch the Earth and bare hands to touch the Earth. If that's not possible, however, don't do it. Sit there and pour love into the Earth, really love the Earth, and sense the Earth as living energy, as living consciousness. Love it, and love it, and love it, and love it. Give it as much love as you possibly can.

Over a period of time, giving love with power, energy, and intention can create a power spot. Once you define a spot, surround it in a bubble of light, and protect it in the bubble of light. Then work with reinforcing and expanding, building and protecting. Without too much effort, in time the spot will be powerful.

Other people coming along would go, "Wooh! Wow! This is a powerful spot!" You can rather just smile gently and say, "Yeah, that's really interesting, isn't it?" Let them think whatever they want to think. Yes, you can create power spots.

If you find one — like the one you found — you can expand it, you can stretch it, or leave it the way it is. If 13 feet is enough, fine, leave it the way it is and work with it. But if you want to stretch it a couple of feet, we would do so. We wouldn't necessarily move a power point once you've found one. "Oh, it would be convenient if it were on the other side of the yard." We'd pretty much leave it where it is. Create it, stretch it, but always respect it.

*Jim Faubel, **Transformation Times**, Beaver Creek, Oregon*

UFOs

Q: There
seems to be a
growing or
escalating
amount of
visual com-
munication
happening
with or from
extraterres-
trials.

Lazaris: Yes,
that's so.

Q: Will it es-
calate even
further?

Lazaris: There will undoubtedly be a time when there will be a proven landing. There have been enough already that are secreted. There is documentation that rather makes it very clear that there are these "extraterrestrials."

Every so often there are what are called the "UFO Flaps" where there are numerous sightings that are seen individually and collectively. In many cases the extraterrestrials are testing. They're rather testing the waters to see if it's safe yet. So far it's been decided that it's not safe, that indeed it would cause just too much turmoil. It would corner people.

Right now people can say, "Ach! Such hogwash! That's silly. That's stupid. There's nothing like that!" But if a craft were to land and people were to get off and photographs were to be taken, even Polaroids, for that matter, we suggest, it would corner people. It would put people in a place where they would have to accept the reality of such beings, and it would throw people into such a turmoil.

The concern of the extraterrestrials is not so much for their safety. The technology that allows travel through time and space certainly isn't going to be bothered by your Earthly weapons. The concern is much more what it would do to you. All the people who don't believe in them would have to confront UFOs right there on the front page of *The New York Times* and on the "CNN Special Report." There would be just such a turmoil on your planet. It would force people into a corner, and they would have to fight, they would have to resist, they would have to do something.

So they test the waters every so often. They try. They see what the response would be.

When they discover that the tenor is such that people won't be too "freaked out," as the term is put, that people can handle it, then there will be a landing. Then there will be quite concrete evidence and finally proof beyond equivocation that such beings exist.

Contact from extraterrestrials is increasing now. Certainly some are here to give advice and to offer insight, but also they're here to learn.

Your planet is going through a New Age. Though the term has been overworked to the point that it is virtually meaningless, there is meaning that lies beneath it, and we suggest that that's a very exciting process for those extraterrestrial beings that are involved in growth as well.

With the birth of a new consciousness, there are a lot of beings — physical and otherwise — that want to gather around and witness that birth. You have noticed that increased interest.

Mary Ellen Pratt & Jack Clarke, New Age Information Network, Atlanta

"With the birth of a new consciousness, there are a lot of beings — physical and otherwise — that want to gather around and witness that birth. You have noticed that increased interest."

Q: Lazaris, please explain a little more about UFO visitors. Do we have a choice about it? Are they capturing people against their will?

Lazaris: No, they are not. We'll just answer that very briefly, and then come back to elaborate. We've talked a little bit about the visitors being here to observe you and to learn from you, perhaps a lot more than they are here to teach you, or to capture you, or anything of that sort.

Now, please understand that there is, in all realities, a continuum. Again, your own self-punishing prejudice against yourselves says that somehow if they are extraterrestrials, then they must all be good, they must all be loving spiritual beings without ego. You assume you're the only ones that have negative ego. We suggest no: The Physical Plane is riddled and rattled and shaken with all kinds of negative ego, and your planet does not have an exclusive on that particular malady, yes?

Other physical beings also have negative egos. Just as it is in the Human Kingdom, on the whole of the Physical Plane there is a continuum. Some people are very, very good, and some people behave very, very badly for reasons of blockages, resistances, and various other things which we shan't go into at this point.

However, there is a continuum. We suggest that other physical planets have the same continuum. Therefore, those that have a grand amount of technology and are able to come and observe your planet, function in that same continuum. Some of them are very, very good, and some of them act and behave very, very badly. Some are arrogant, unbelievably arrogant, in that sense. Floating around in their little space ships, they think they're so much better than everybody else — you and their own brethren for that matter.

We suggest that, yes, there are some that rather look at you as though you're animals to be tested, not unlike the way you look at chimpanzees, mice, rats, and various other test animals. Those extraterrestrials think that it's for the greater good of humanity, and therefore it doesn't matter if they do this to you or do that to you. Some wouldn't mind at all or would see no problem with picking you up and operating on you and testing you just to see how you tick.

They are a slim minority, a very slim minority. The vast majority wouldn't even consider such activity, for they realize that you are humanity as well — not in the same form as they, but you are humanity as well. You have feelings. They know that.

You are coming to learn that animals have feelings. Whatever your philosophy about animal testing, all of you are at least reevaluating which tests should and should not be done with animals.

The difference, however, between you and animals is that you are human and those E.T.s who would be observing you are also of the Human Kingdom — not human beings, but of the Human Kingdom. Therefore, you create your reality, and, therefore, no: There is not a single person who has honestly ever been abducted who has not been so abducted for reasons of compliance *on some level*. It may not be on a level of which they are consciously aware. They may not *cause* it, but they are *allowing* the reality. They have agreed, on some level. They have allowed that reality, on some level. For whatever reason, they said that it was all right with them to be abducted. They may now regret the allowed abduction; however, whatever they think they went through was part of their own creation, absolutely so.

If you don't want to be picked up, you won't be, clearly. Absolutely not. Clearly, absolutely not. So you don't have to be afraid if an E.T. comes into your back yard that somehow you're going to be abducted against your will. It just will not happen.

"There is not a single person who has honestly ever been abducted who has not been so abducted for reasons of compliance on some level."

Even if they're malevolent, you create your own reality! Therefore, it's got to be your agreement that you would be so abducted.

Additionally, we suggest that one must understand that there are all kinds of extraterrestrials. There are all kinds of UFOs. Some of them are from different planetary systems within your universe; some of them are from different planetary systems outside your universe.

We also suggest that some of what you call UFOs are the future intersecting with your present, or slipping through a time warp into your present. Therefore, what some may observe as an unidentified flying object may truly be a future aircraft of the United States Air Force.

It might be a plane or traveling craft that is from the year 2350 A.D. that has slipped through a time warp and streaks across your skies in 1988, and then, in a flash, returns to its reality. On some of your late-night — "red eye special" — flights, can you say for sure you do not "slip" into the 1930s or 1940s? Perhaps your 747s of today are your grandparents' UFOs of yesterday. Don't be so sure!

Now that's a little mind-boggling, we understand, for some of you. "Wait a minute! Wait a minute!" But all time is simultaneous. Every past, every present, every future exists simultaneously.

"... what some may observe as an unidentified flying object may truly be a future aircraft of the United States Air Force."

Therefore, in the future they're going to learn to time travel. They have learned it already in the future! When you catch up there, you will learn how to time travel. We suggest some of them are time traveling into the past — just as in the various stories you have, such as "Back to the Future," and the time travel tales from H. G. Wells, or whatever.

Where do you think those ideas came from? Do you think those people just made it up out of nothing? No, in that sense, they grasped hold of a piece of the future and brought it into their present to write about going from their present into a distant past.

There will be a time when time travel does occur, and when that does happen, sometimes they have time warps, and they slip through and zip right through your reality. "I've never seen a craft like that." That's right. You won't probably see it for another 300 years or so. In that sensing, sometimes they are that. It's a UFO!

Some of the extraterrestrials or unidentified flying objects are products of mass consciousness. At one time you, as a humanity, created a god in your own image. The primitive people of religion created their gods to be pretty nasty sorts of characters. Some would say that the original God of your Old Testament was one pretty nasty sort of guy. … {laughter} … According to that Testament, many were killed in the name of God. According to history many more were killed in His name.

Who really did that? Was it really God? Or was it … "Hey, I spoke to God last night, and God told me to kill you." … {laughter} … "If I don't want to be responsible, I'll blame the big man upstairs," yes?

Nonetheless, the doctrines that have been put forth rather depict this very arbitary, very grudge-holding sort of energy. Remember now that this is the god who said that because one woman ate one apple, all women for all time must suffer. … {laughter} … Now there's not a human being on the planet that carries a grudge that long … {laughter} … This is also the God that said that you must suffer the sins of the father for three or four generations. Now how long is that, if 30 years is a generation? And four generations is 120 years. There's your father — that's one — your grandfather — two — great grandfather is three … However many it is, if they sinned, you've got to pay for it. Now that's holding a grudge a bit long. … {laughter} …

But you see, that's what the people wanted. They wanted a god that would do their bidding. It wasn't God/Goddess/All That Is; it was the people who claimed to speak for God.

"You want to have a God. Some people now want to turn computers into their gods. Others want to turn extraterrestrials, with their tremendous technological knowledge, into their god. There are those people who create the hysteria of seeing UFOs, and they are purely manifestations, subjective manifestations, of an archetypal energy that resides within them."

Then people changed, and they shifted, and along came an opening up to the possibility of creating the future and changing all that. And how did that change?

Well, God sent his only begotten Son to give the New Testament, the new law. According to the New Testament, Jesus came for your sins, but he also brought the new law.

The New Testament says the new law replaces the Ten Commandments. That was the thing: Replacing those Ten Commandments here's one new law. Simple. Love God above all others, and love others as you would love yourself. And all of a sudden God became much more compassionate.

Well then, as you move forward, the faces — the images — of God keep changing. Many of you remember, in the Sixties there was the "God is dead" activity, when people became rather cynical, scared, and angry that the world was not turning out to be this "heaven" that they had been promised by their technocrats. When the promise was broken, the promise that you could have anything and everything you wanted, people said, "God is dead." Others said, "There never was one in the first place."

Well, you are, as we say, a spiritual nation. You want to have a God. Some people now want to turn computers into their gods. Others want to turn extraterrestrials, with their tremendous technological knowledge, into their god. There are those people who create the hysteria of seeing UFOs, which are purely manifestations, subjective manifestations, of an archetypal energy that resides within them. In this case, which is frequent — too frequent — UFOs are subjective archetypal "faces of God" created in a high-tech image of a high-tech society.

Quite honestly, this category of UFO does more of the "abducting" than any other. Those people who have a belief and a fear that there are extraterrestrials who are going to abduct them, who are going to run tubes up various parts of their bodies ... {laughter} ... and who are going to have sex with them in some sort of weird way ... {laughter} ... are more likely to attract a conscious manifestation of a subconscious subjective archetype. Such subjective archetypal manifestations can take on the projection of a "god" who is arbitrary or cruel, one who might look on a human being as just some animal to be tested — an object to be used.

You see, you have no real concept of how incredibly powerful your brain is. You know, they tell you that you use 10% of your brain. That's really incorrect. You use 100% of your brain. You only understand 10%. The other 90% is still functioning, and the other 90% can spin out a reality — and sometimes a very negative reality — that you experience as being as real, *as physically real*, as any other.

Your brain is not the passive receiver it was once thought to be. It is not the passive receiver that many want to pretend it still is. Your brain is an active searcher involved in what we call "future-think." Even though you may not totally understand how it functions, that other 90% of your brain can create and manifest reality. And even though you may not totally understand it, it is still a conscious choice because you are allowing it, consciously allowing it. You just don't always understand how. Not yet, at least.

Now you know, for example, that with hypnosis you can tell a person, when you touch them with a pencil, that it is a burning cigarette. You can touch their arm, and that place will welt, blister, and burn, as though you really did it with a cigarette. You know that. That's been demonstrated sufficiently and adequately. You can hypnotize someone to tell them that they are in severe danger, or that they are in total safety, and they will respond completely and totally.

No one fully knows what they are seeing. No one fully knows what they're experiencing. Even when they recall, it's sometimes impossible to know. Therefore, we suggest, your brain is capable of doing this kind of activity to the body. Therefore, you are capable, as human beings, of taking subjective archetypes and manifesting them objectively. The holographic imagery can look to you as though it's three-dimensional, solid and real reality, when it is truly an apparition. It is a subconscious archetypal energy manifesting conscious reality. This can happen for one person. "But I saw it, too!" It can happen for many, many people.

An example is one of the most powerful mystics in your world in her time — her time (we said that correctly) — H. P. Blavatsky, who could teleport herself from one room to another. In her personal diaries, what she talked of was really her ability to hypnotize an entire room of people to believe that she disappeared. Then she moved into an entirely different room and appeared there. Her capacity to mass hypnotize in that way was incredible.

There are ways in which people can hypnotize themselves to see what they want to see or what they believe they see. And it is, in a sense, a hysterical manifestation — not bizarre hysterical — but a hysterical manifestation of a subjective archetypal energy in a conscious form. That happens — not all the time — but that's a part of what happens.

There are many kinds of extraterrestrials: friendly and not so friendly, teachers, but mainly observers, physical futures warping into the present, and conscious manifestations of subconscious subjective archetypes. There are real E.T.s, and there are imaginary ones.

No matter the kind, in a roundabout way, no, you need not be afraid of being abducted and treated badly unless there's a part of you, maybe a very secret part of you, that would kind of "get off on it." ... {laughter} ...

All right ...

Anonymous Question, Evening with Lazaris, Atlanta, 1988

Crystals

Q: Could you speak a little bit about crystals and their powers?

Lazaris: Many minerals, many rocks and stones and pieces of metal, for that matter, have very beautiful, powerful properties, and they can be used in a similar sense as a crystal. But the difference is that a crystal is more geared to be so used as a power object, as a focus of attention, as a lens, so to speak, of magnifying energy, as a natural "laser-like" energy. The beauty of a crystal is based on several factors:

The first factor is its piezoelectric quality, where the electrons that are on the surface are easily released and regathered. Through squeezing a crystal, light emanates, and with the light, energy. When one programs a crystal, as we call it, or implants it or impregnates it with knowledge, that knowledge can be released, or it can be retained within the crystal because of the electron structure and because of the latticework spiral molecular structure of the crystal.

Therefore, energy that is put within it in the form of light, in the form of consciousness, can then be released through squeezing, through the pressure. That energy can be regathered once again. The molecular structure, the function of the electrons, and the piezo-electric energy of crystals make them conducive to amplifying energy. In addition, silicon is a semiconductor, and because of the amount of silicon in the crystal, it can work very handily to hold or to release energy.

A conductor is a substance that conducts electricity. A nonconductor is a substance that doesn't conduct. A semiconductor sometimes conducts and sometimes does not conduct electricity. The function of a semiconductor allows the entire binary computerized system to work. It is quite phenomenal in your world. A crystal has that same capacity, and therefore it can hold energy or release it.

It is a semiconductor, and, therefore, when you put a thought, any thought, positive or negative, into a crystal, it can be held there indefinitely, and it can be released indefinitely. When you combine together the two properties of piezoelectric energy and of holding and releasing thought through the silicon properties, you've got a very, very special mineral here that indeed can be tremendously useful as a tool.

"A crystal does not create energy. It simply amplifies the energy that it is given, releases it upon cue, and gathers it upon cue. People can make a mistake with crystals by giving their power away to them."

A crystal does not create energy. It simply amplifies the energy that it is given, releases it upon cue, and gathers it upon cue. People can make a mistake with crystals by giving their power away to them. "The crystals did it. The crystals are this. The crystals are that." No, they are tools. They are servants of yours. They are here to be used and to be used beautifully, hopefully for the betterment of yourself and those around you, but they are tools nonetheless, and they would not want to be anything more.

"They are here to be used and to be used beautifully, hopefully for the betterment of yourself and those around you, but they are tools nonetheless, and they would not want to be anything more."

As you learn to work with crystals, as you learn, as you experiment and explore, not only will you learn from what you read in books, but also you will learn from your own experience. Your experience superbly teaches you how to most effectively use a crystal for yourself.

Also, we would add that some people will be intimately drawn to crystals, and they will have a natural instinct, a natural ability, when it comes to working with crystals. Others, in that sense, may hold a crystal, roll it around in their hand, squeeze it, and try to work with it, only to find it's ... ah, nothing but a clear piece of stone to them. Some people just don't have an affinity for them. It doesn't mean the crystals aren't right, and it doesn't mean the person isn't right. It just means that there is not a union between the two, and therefore don't bother. Don't try to force yourself. Don't try to make a tool that doesn't fit your hand work for you.

If you find you have a natural affinity, use it. Learn from books, but develop and trust your own instinct and experience. The proper way to use crystals is to use them in the way they work best — for you.

Crystals are increasingly powerful tools. They were used very powerfully in Lemuria and Atlantis, whether you believe in those civilizations or not. As the New Age unfolds — more importantly, as the energy of the New Age arises — the value and the use of crystals will increase.

"As people will work with crystals, realizing that they are tools of growth, not the leaders of growth, they will come to realize that they are not just "working" with crystals; they are also guardians of crystals."

There will be a great deal of scientific investigation proving very clearly that crystals have a tremendous amount of positive impact and potential, depending upon the attitude with which they're used. As people will work with crystals, realizing that they are tools of growth, not the leaders of growth, they will come to realize that they are not just "working" with crystals; they are also guardians of crystals.

No one can own a crystal, for a crystal has its own consciousness, alive and vibrant. You can be a guardian, and it can serve you well, for whatever length of time you hold it, for whatever length of time you are its guardian.

At some time, you will pass them on, either as a part of your estate — hopefully people who hold crystals will take that responsibility — or as gifts. It is appropriate to pass those crystals on to new guardians, or to potentially return them to the Earth from whence they came, to free them to their own growth, to their own consciousness. As you approach crystals from this point of view, they can take on a whole personality, as well as an entire consciousness.

*David Rogers, **Llewellyn's New Times**, St. Paul, Minnesota*

Address to the First Annual Crystal Congress 1987

"... in time there will be greater understanding and appreciation. Crystals will not be just an ornamentation; they will be powerful, powerful generators of the two most important energies you've got: love and light."

Lazaris: And so it is a pleasure to be greeting you and to be talking with you, albeit briefly, today. You each have a variety of backgrounds. In this lifetime alone, as you look around you, you see many with whom you will agree and some with whom you will disagree as to the importance and the particular uses of these rather strange and phenomenal substances called crystals. You have differing philosophies and understandings of metaphysics and spirituality and even a variety of personal philosophies that run the gamut, most definitely so.

But there is one thing that you all agree upon, and that is that crystals are important, yes? Crystals are valuable. Indeed crystals are increasing in their esoteric value exponentially as this century comes to a close, as this Old Age of spirituality and metaphysical understanding comes to its conclusion to open to a New Age, a New Spirituality, and a New Metaphysics.

You all agree that the crystal will play an important role in that unfoldment, for that is why you have gathered at this convention. That is why you have come together with all your diversity, with all your differing opinions, with all your differing attitudes — to share, to learn, to teach, to study. You all are guardians of a truth that is now unfolding more than ever.

We are not here to tell you how to use your crystals — no, not at all. We're not here to tell you how important they are, what they're made of, and what their chemical balances mean. No, not at all. Indeed, we respect your knowledge. We respect your demonstrated dedication to these wondrous little creatures called crystals.

No, you are here to do all of that together. We're here to talk to you about something, perhaps to remind you of something.

You have a role in the unfolding future. You have a role as guardians of crystals. You have a role as the keepers of knowledge and the sharers of that knowledge as this Age unfolds.

Some of you think crystals are for healing only, and some say, "No, it's not for that at all." Others find crystal balls, some find candles and spheres, and yet others find differing shapes to be more or less valuable.

If you get together to explain your differences, you will be here for a very long, long time. Rather, gather to share your alikeness, gather to share your understandings, in order to build a base, a foundation, as to the value of the crystal. We're here to remind you of the delicate relationship between the crystals you hold and the guardians you are.

Crystals, as you realize, have many purposes, many reasons for being. Among those purposes, crystals gather and disseminate energy vibration and understanding. They communicate. Through the harmony and balance they provide, crystals also play a role in protecting and healing.

Similarly, crystals have this wonderful ability to amplify energy that can be projected into the past, present, and the future — that can be directed in any way you desire — for your purposes, with harm to none, in order to manifest a more glorious reality and a more positive and powerful future. In this amplification, they can focus, by condensing or expanding understanding, and condensing or expanding awareness.

Crystals, therefore, are an integral part of what is called the transmutation of energy for the transformation of consciousness. These functions are core to the very essence of the mineral: to balance, to gather, to amplify, to transmute and transform, to focus through condensing and expanding, to communicate through the morphogenic process of transmitting understanding and knowledge, and to heal and protect.

No matter what crystal techniques you favor, these are the core essences, these are the core elements of what the crystal is about. For what reason are you using technique? Is it not for the same purpose? Crystals and the techniques you use have the same end: to bring balance and harmony, to gather, to release and amplify, to transmute/transform, to focus, to teach and communicate, and to heal.

Now let's look at you, the guardian. Like the crystals and the techniques, your function is also the same. First, you are not owners, but guardians, of these very special creatures, these very special consciousnesses, these very special lights that are frozen in time and space. Crystals are tools to be used by and for you to fulfill your work and to fulfill their purpose. You have become physical, and you have come to this First Crystal Congress to balance, to gather together your understanding and your information, to amplify your sameness and to transmute/transform your differences, to focus, to communciate, to heal and protect. You plan to gather and store all of this in your body. Then you will release what you have gathered when appropriate.

You have come to this Congress to transmute your energy for the purposes of transforming your reality and the reality of the consensus reality as well. You are here to focus by condensing your thought and your awareness and by expanding your understanding and your acceptance of each other. You plan to communciate. One by one you will leave and go home, back to your world, back to your own surroundings. As you communicate to one, and one to another, and another to one, you function to heal the planet, to heal a society, to heal a world, to heal a future.

Therefore, you and crystals have something very much in common in that your work is the same. You perform it differently, but you are partners. You are partners together in this reality creation of your world. As part of your destiny, if you will, you have chosen to use these various wonderful minerals. You have also agreed to be the guardians — the legs, the hands, the body — for that knowledge that is frozen in time and in space, so that the crystals might do the work that they are now coming to the surface to do.

You are here not just as guardians, not just as conduits, not just as those that will carry the crystals about from place to place; you are here to do *your* work as well. Your work and the crystals' work being one is what has drawn you together, what has brought you, with your interest, with your fascination, with your wonder and your curiosity to honor crystals.

Whereas others might see them as simply pretty stones, you see them as alive, living, beautiful consciousnesses because you are seeing yourself in them. You are seeing your work and your destiny reflected back to you. Therefore, accept the destiny of the crystal, and accept your destiny as well, and bring these two together to personally establish the balance and harmony, to personally gather and store and release, when it is appropriate, to personally amplify, to transmute and transform, to communicate, to focus, and to heal.

Despite your diversities, despite your personal differences, despite what you may disagree upon, come together on this, your destiny. Come together on this, the importance and value of the crystals, by whatever use or method, for those Doomers and Gloomers who are so quick to say it's over are not counting on you, are not making allowances for your presence, nor for the power of the crystals that you guardian.

You are the light. You are the beacons for a future that can be. In your daily routine, in the larger scope of what you are doing, see the importance of you and the value of your work as you stretch and reach to understand, as you stretch and reach to learn, as you stretch and reach to teach and to be taught.

Over the next many years, crystal technology will increase, as will the interest of the world-at-large. Initially there will be the few, the dedicated, and then there will be onlookers and those who are intrigued and excited for reasons they cannot even begin to understand.

And then there will be the serious skeptic. All this has already happened and is happening even still.

This circus will develop out of those who will jump on a bandwagon for their own personal gain and for their own personal financial futures and expressions. Amidst it all, there will be those such as you who love the energy that is a crystal, that sense them like living beings, who understand them in ways that others cannot begin to sense.

The circus will dance around you as you proceed step by step. There will be those with outlandish ideas of what can be done with these wonderful creatures, and those with very limited views. But step by step you will move forward, and in time there will be greater understanding and appreciation. Crystals will not be just an ornamentation; they will be powerful, powerful generators of the two most important energies you've got: love and light.

That generation of love and light will happen esoterically, and it will also happen much more practically as people use crystals in practical appliances and radionic devices. The importance and the value of crystals will rise, will be discovered, will come forth "initially" and again, and you are a part of that.

By your destiny, by your decision to bring forth this understanding, to bring forth this knowledge, you are a part of this unfolding. Value yourself and your play. Value your part in the unfolding of this New Age, this New Spirituality, this new destiny. When the circus ends, and those who were involved just for the faddishness, just for the glamour and glitter, go home or off to some other twinkling bauble of metaphysical awareness, those who are left — yourselves — will offer to your world answers through the crystals that you love.

So it is that we have enjoyed talking with you, albeit briefly, today, to congratulate you for coming together as a body to share, to learn, to study, to work, to become the very crystals you love, and to love the very crystals you've become.

We close, with love ... and peace.

The Crystal Congress, Los Angeles, 1987

The Brain & Consciousness

Lazaris: The fluids in the ventricles are conducting and semiconducting. There is a sense of the soul/spirit interfacing with the brain and mind. This is the common ground where the barriers between levels of consciousness are dissolved.

Consciousness enters in the fourth ventricle. All the ventricles are revolving doorways where consciousness enters physicality. Through the self-generated revolving doors a circular, whirling energy draws information in and pushes it out.

It is like a crystal cave, almost circular like a geode. Multifaceted tiny crystalline points act somewhat like such semiconductors as silicon. A thick, structured spiraling latticework of fluid — an electric fluid energy — holds and releases data.

The ventricles are involved in feelings. Joy, wonder and curiosity are light vibrations of different frequencies. Happiness, for example, sets off frequencies throughout the body into the nervous sytem and the ventricles. It then influences and colors thought. It sets up somewhat holographically the screen that captures the thought. The feelings change the vibrations and therefore the reality. The picture changes as a reference beam and an illuminating beam come into phase, creating apparent physicality.

The body is also a hologram. So who is the viewer? One's Higher Consciousness or Future Self is doing the watching. One of the viewing screens is in the brain's ventricles.

The vibrational frequencies are set up from future choices that come into the present against the backdrop

Q: We've been speculating that the brain ventricles (four connected cavities filled with cerebrospinal fluid) may be involved in mediating consciousness? Any comment?

of the past. The ventricles are not only information exchanges from one level to another, but also from one time to another.

Linear time is a manmade illusion. The effect in the chosen future leads to the cause in the present. As you decide what you are going to become, the choice influences what you are.

Marilyn Ferguson, **Brain/Mind Bulletin**, *October, 1987*

Meditation

Q: Would you mind giving your views on the importance and use of meditation?

Lazaris: Certainly so. Well, we could perhaps talk for hours and hours about the subject of meditation, because it is such a critically important part of what would be called the New Age. It is an integral part of one's personal and private Spiritual Journey Home.

We would suggest that meditation, by whatever definition, is basically "getting out of the way." It is altering your state of consciousness. From the simplest action of closing your eyes (which alters your state of consciousness), to the very intricate and complex action of entering deeper and deeper and more profound levels of mind through body posture, through breathing techniques, or through visualization techniques, meditation is a powerful and varied way of altering your state of consciousness.

First, when you use meditation you can step outside of time and space. We like to say that you can walk between time, that you can slip between space.

In those altered states of consciousness, between time and space, you are able to accomplish a tremendous amount of change, a tremendous amount of growth. What might, in a therapeutic setting, take months and even years to change can be done in a series of meditations very easily, because you are functioning outside of time and space, and therefore it doesn't have to take six months or six years.

This is not to suggest that those traditional therapies aren't helpful. In fact, we suggest, take the advantages of traditional therapy or humanistic therapy and use them in a meditative setting.

You're gaining the best of both worlds in that you are stepping outside of time and space, and using psychologically sound techniques and approaches to alter your perspective and your reality. Meditation is very useful in that it speeds up your process — it allows you to grow much faster, much more effectively, much more powerfully.

Secondly, meditation opens you up to the other levels of your mind. You are aware of a conscious self, very much so. Everyone is aware of it to one degree or another.

There is also a subconscious, and as we call it, an unconscious, and indeed a Higher Conscious Mind. Access to these minds can happen spontaneously, admittedly so. When it is spontaneous it is very beautiful, very exciting, and is often referred to as an "enlightenment experience." Sometimes it's called a "peak experience" according to Abraham Maslow.

With meditation you can direct, and you can decide when you're going to have those peak experiences. You can decide when you're going to have those enlightenment moments. You don't have to wait for them to occur spontaneously.

And therefore, Tuesday afternoon at 3:00 you can sit down, close your eyes, go through a particular meditative process, and connect with your subconscious, unconscious, or Higher Conscious self and grow, reach, stretch, understand, and make changes. Access to the other worlds clearly is a tremendous benefit of meditation.

"Those of you who inspire others and work as inspirations in the world need to be retuned. Meditation can provide the healing process for that retuning, retoning and recharging."

Thirdly, metaphysical/spiritual techniques can be done in meditation far more effectively, far more powerfully than they can be done with eyes-open interaction with the Physical Plane. Meditation provides a tremendous environment, a tremendous set and setting, in which to allow the cultivation of metaphysical/spiritual concepts. Meditation can provide something of a greenhouse effect where it can stimulate and augment the growth of those metaphysical and spiritual concepts.

Finally, in the hecticness of your world, and in the Rubik's Cube reality that seems to have no solutions, you can get very scattered. Those of you who inspire others and work as inspirations in the world need to be retuned. Meditation can provide the healing process for that retuning, retoning and recharging.

Now we have suggested four values and uses of meditation: (1) You can step between time and space and grow spiritually and psychologically much faster; (2) you can work with other levels of your consciousness; (3) you can apply metaphysical and spiritual techniques as well as psychological techniques more effectively, more fervently and more powerfully; and (4) indeed you can retune, recharge and retone yourself in a healing process. Those are four. The values of meditation are endless. We list these four primarily because they're the foundation from which other benefits can spring in using meditation to grow, to stretch, to reach, to become more of who you are. You can use meditation to attain that sense of God/Goddess/All That Is that is within each of you and is beyond each of you, too.

Lee Perry, Van Nuys, California

L azaris: Have a ball with it, yes ... No, we have considered and decided no, we would not make movies of our meditations. We have made this decision for one very important reason.

Your imagination is incredibly powerful. As we talked in the weekend, the brain has developed so spectacularly, for it is also growing — it is also expanding. It has developed so spectacularly that your capacity to imagine now is so much more vivid, so much more powerful, so much more beautiful than what it was 200, 300 or 500 years ago.

As we suggest that now, because of television, because of radio, and because of books, you have exercised the imaging part of the brain, and you have developed it so beautifully. Therefore, in a meditation when you sense a forest or you sense a beach at night, your capacity to imagine that, to experience that, is quite incredible.

If indeed we were to translate those meditations into a script of some sort, it would be the director's, it would be the special effects person's, it would be the technician's ... It would be *their* image of what we said rather than *your* image of what we said.

This is why very clearly we say: Do not share the context and the form of your meditation, only the con-

Q: The imagery in your guided meditations is very beautiful and vivid. Have you ever thought of making a movie of your meditations such as the Causal Plane Meditation? The Hollywood special effects and computer-generated graphics people would have a ball with it.

tent, because if you share the context and the form, it only ends up hurting people — either yourself because it's not as good as somebody else's, or somebody else because it's not as good as yours.

The context and the form is what you generate consciously, each of you individually. Certain artists with whom we talk and who come to workshops have, from time to time, attempted to paint the Causal Plane or this meditation or that meditation, for example. And though they heard exactly the same words, most other people could not recognize it.

"What's that?"

"That's the Causal Plane."

"No. That's not what it looks like to me." ... {laughter} ...

"That's the Altar of Forgiveness."

"That's not the way mine looks." ... {laughter} ...

And then self-doubt: "Or should it?" ... {laughter} ... "Uh-oh, mine wasn't right. That's probably the right way, the way it should have looked. I failed." You see? Suppose the movie comes out. "That's not how it looked at all! That's not the way I saw it." Indeed, the book in your head was much better than the movie on the screen.

Now, we are working with certain people who are writers and with certain movie industry people. With some of these people we have worked quite extensively. When they are writing and rewriting, we offer suggestions and ideas to include and not include. To that extent we are definitely an influence in that particular medium, and it's fun, and that's exactly why we're doing it.

It's not necessary. It's fun.

Anonymous Question, Evening with Lazaris, Atlanta, 1987

Harmonic Convergence

Lazaris: Well, you know, reality-altering possibilities open up when each person allows themselves to have vision. We have talked since November of 1986 very directly — and before that more abstractly — that what's important for the future, in order to find the solutions to these problems that so many are telling you are solutionless, is to develop, first, a personal vision, a private vision of what you see for yourself, what you see for your future.

Q: Harmonic Convergence, as it's being called, is happening in August (1987) What do you see coming up for us in the way of reality-altering possibilities?

Secondly, develop a public vision, a world vision, of what you see in the future — a vision of the peace, the harmony and the beauty of a world that is to come. Though your vision may not include a specific solution to a specific issue, you can see it done without understanding exactly how to generate that solution.

We suggest that when you see it done, when you see it already complete, it puts forth healing and creating energy into the cosmos so as to allow those solutions to come forward. Even though you don't know the solutions, you can create others having the dreams, finding the solutions through *your* vision.

Each person needs to converge their energy. Each person needs now to focus and to set priorities. You need to remind yourselves of your particular destiny in this unfolding world of yours.

If each of you does that individually, you will perform a miraculously wonderful convergence of the human consciousness and a convergence of that future. That a particular time is being set aside in accordance with a certain calendar is wonderful.

A date has been picked where groups of people working in harmony, working together in what we call synergy, will each personally provide the convergence. That, we suggest, can have a monumental impact.

The impact of Harmonic Convergence will *not* be such that on the day after you'll notice that all of a sudden the skies are bluer, and the waters are purer, and the air is less polluted. But in a larger picture, in the broader scope, we suggest that a significant shift will have begun. Like a trim tab, a slight movement of energy will ultimately produce a major change in the course and the direction of the future. That subtle-to-obvious shift will be positive.

*Van Ault, **Magical Blend**, January 1988*

Q: When this interview is published the Harmonic Convergence will be over, but can you tell us more about the significance of this event and where we go from here?

Lazaris: Well, indeed, there are many who will have differing opinions: "What was that thing in the middle of August after all?" Some are sure that it's an "ending of" or a "beginning of." We suggest that according to the Mayan calendar, it is a time of change. It is a time of "a jump," as some people are putting it. Perhaps it is a time of the quantum jump, a quantum leap forward in the growth, in the evolution, in the expansion of consciousness. It is a totally positive event.

Even though many will be frightened by it or will want to see the fear of it, it is a totally positive event. It is a time that you as a humanity, you as a consciousness, in a sense, speed up, speed up your process, speed up your growth, expand your awareness.

It is also a time when you "converge," when you "bring together." Looking in the dictionary for the meaning of the word, *to converge* means to bring together the different components of yourself.

Therefore, it was and still is a time of important change. Those dates, August 16, 17 and 18, 1987, have passed, and the energy is still there and will be with you for many, many years yet to come. It is a time when you need to prioritize, to pull together: "What are my talents? What are my abilities? What are my creative energies? What are my purposes? What are my focuses (as we refer to them)? Why am I here? What do I want to accomplish, and how do I want to accomplish it?"

"It is a time that you take your power back ... a time that you emerge as the creator of your own reality consciously."

Answer questions, these and others, and pull the answers together. Converge your energy, bringing together your varying thoughts and ideas and feelings that hitherto in your day-in and day-out reality seem to get scattered all over the place.

Bring them together, and align them — align them in harmony with each other so that your talents, creativity, desires of what you *want* to accomplish, your abilities of what you *can* accomplish, and your hopes, dreams, and expectations all line up. Bring them into an alignment on those days. Still, even though these specific days in August have passed, continue to align. Demand, declare, and project the future, the positive, loving, caring, healing future that you want.

This is a time when the convergence can happen, a Harmonic Convergence where you can shift from what has been called the "Doom and Gloom" into a brand new "bloom." You can shift your world so the future isn't one of destruction. The future can be budding and new. Your world can open itself to brand new and very powerful and beautiful potentials. This is a time when you can get on one side of the fence or the other.

The convergence happens on more than just three days. "Oh, I missed it! It's too bad!" No. You are on time. It is now and for the remainder of your century.

The more you can state your position, the more you can get on one side of the fence or the other, and the more you start honestly generating the reality that you expect for the future, and the more power you have.

That's what the Harmonic Convergence is about: It is a time that you take your power back, even from those prognosticators from thousands of years ago, a time that you emerge as the creator of your own reality consciously. And that's what the Harmonic Convergence and the subsequent Emergence is all about.

*Jim Faubel, **Transformation Times**, Beaver Creek, Oregon*

Q: Will the Harmonic Convergence result in a greater gulf between those who are striving to raise their consciousness and those who are not?

Lazaris: From one perspective, yes, there will be a greater gulf. In a sense, there will be the chasm widening. There will be an overall increase in those who are seeking spirituality, but the chasm will widen between whether that spirituality is sought in a Fundamentalist or traditional sense, or whether it's found in a new and alternative sense.

With this gulf, it's not as though people will become enlightened or unenlightened so much as people will seek more and more spirituality in more and more ways. Some will seek it through metaphysics and the New Spirituality. Others will turn to the spirituality of their childhood, to the traditions and to the Fundamentalists, and therefore all forms of spirituality will increase.

In your world now, with an increase in television evangelism and the various other evangelical and pentecostal movements, people are turning more and more to seeking and trying to find a God. Though there will be an increasing gulf, both sides of that gulf will also increase.

As the convergence occurs, yes, there will be a greater split — but it will not be something that you'll notice the next day, and then all of a sudden you're aware: "Where have all the Fundamentalists gone?" Or, "Where have all the Mystics gone?" No. It won't be that obvious, but over the time period one can look back and see that yes, there was a change that occurred somewhere there in August of 1987.

Lazaris: There are people who are rather critical of *The Mayan Factor*, suggesting that Jose Arguelles' mathematics are off, and they offer other criticisms. We're not so much concerned with those sorts of details. What we are concerned with is that yes, indeed, in that time of August 16 and 17 for the two days and the nine days actually (from August 16 and 17 to August 24), there was a shift of energy that did occur. And this shift extends from this year of 1987 for a period of 5 years, and 25 years. There was a shift of consciousness that did occur.

Q: In a recent workshop you stated that the Harmonic Convergence happened in the hope that something would change. Did something really change?

Now admittedly there were those that were expecting that shift to be much grander, that were expecting UFOs to come in formation, or to land in some stadium somewhere, or something like that. There were those who expected that teleportation and levitation would somehow all of a sudden become prevalent. Those people who expected such were correctly disappointed. They should never have expected such things in the first place.

What did happen, however, was that there was a focus of energy, there was a converging, as the term has been put, of personal energies, group energies, and even global energies. The words sound so simple; their impact can be grand.

Harmonic Convergence was a beginning of an energy of working together. There is an energy of working together to build the energy that is *between*.

As we look at it, all of metaphysics has talked of the energy *within*, rightly and correctly so, and hopefully you will continue to speak of it. There is also an energy that is developed *together* — obviously, "as two or more gather."

There is additionally an energy that is the energy that is *between*. As people work together, certainly so, they combine the energy that is *within* with the energy that is *together* to create an energy that is *between*.

Now the terms may seem rather interchangeable, but there's a difference. What it means is:

(1) An acceleration of growth.

(2) Positive energy and positive results that will show up in the next several years.

(3) An increasing number of people who will find themselves drawn into the arena of metaphysics and to the New Spirituality that it represents.

Did something really change? Yes. Is that change real? That's up to you … each of you.

*Cindy Saul, **PhenomeNEWS**, Southfield, Michigan*

Atlantis & Lemuria

Lazaris: The energy that was and is Lemuria is re-emerging. Edgar Cayce many years ago suggested in one of his predictions that Atlantis would once again rise, and to look to the latter part of the 1960s. 1968 was often the year mentioned. Many enthusiasts, with their binoculars and their boats, went out looking for the reemergence of Atlantis. They interpreted Cayce literally, and expected a land mass to rise out of the ocean.

Q: Would you discuss the major focus of Lemuria, and anything else about Lemuria that might benefit?

No, his prediction was symbolic, and basically what he was saying in that prediction was that the interest and the energy of that which is symbolically the continent of Atlantis would once again emerge in the late 1960s. The Human Potential Movement and the Metaphysical Potential Movement, indicative of the late 1960s, 1970s and into the early 1980s, is the reemergence of the energy of Atlantis. Cayce was correct, if interpreted properly.

We have suggested that Lemuria will once again re-emerge. But do not get boats, and do not go looking in the Pacific, because there's no land mass that is going to show up, not at all. No, Lemuria is an energy, and we would suggest, the energy of Lemuria will reemerge. Lemuria is a state of mind. That state of mind will re-emerge.

Lemuria was, indeed, a civilization, but you'll never be able to prove it. It lies beyond what we call the Bridge of Belief. In order for Lemuria to be real, it must be something you believe, not something that you concretely prove — just as Atlantis can never be technically proved — just as, in that sense, God/Goddess/All That

Is will never be proved. All must lie beyond The Bridge of Belief, because the magic and the mystery of each requires the energy of believing, not the energy of empirical proving.

We call Lemuria "The Land That Imagination Forgot," and it is now the time of its reemergence. Lemuria symbolizes the reemergence of imagination, the reemergence of feeling, and the reemergence of creating through conceptual/mental processes. The reemergence of Lemuria is using meditation and programming — using technique and processing — to conceive and perceive the world as a reality that you can create — that you can consciously create.

"The Human Potential Movement and the Metaphysical Potential Movement are connected to Atlantis; we would suggest the Spiritual Potential Movement is connected to Lemuria."

The Human Potential Movement and the Metaphysical Potential Movement are connected to Atlantis; we would suggest the Spiritual Potential Movement is connected to Lemuria. Lemuria is a state of mind. It is the reemergence of the Goddess energy. It is the reemergence of the feminine energy — not of womanhood, but of feminine energy.

"Lemuria is a state of mind. It is the reemergence of the Goddess energy. It is the reemergence of the feminine energy — not of womanhood, but of feminine energy."

The reemergence is a time when people are going to learn to love in the real sense of what the word means. Love will be more than just a four-letter word to throw around to make others feel guilty, or to manipulate others. It will become a real energy of giving, of responding, of respecting, of knowing, of being intimate, of being committed, and of caring — really caring. This real energy of love will provide certain beautiful qualities of security, pleasure, safety and trust. It will also reduce the fears of loss, give a sense of intimacy and caring, and offer a sense of knowing.

The reemergence of Lemuria will mark the beginning of a world that begins to work together, that begins to work together not in the old sense of "together," not in the old sense of "group," where people use group to hide out, but in the new sense of group where people legitimately bring their value, their skill, their ability, their talent, their creativity, and their productivity to work together.

The reemergence of the energy of Lemuria is happening. It's going to provide many of the answers to the problems that seem to have no answers, many of the solutions to the conundrums of your reality.

The answers will come *through* that energy. Lemuria, the energy that imagination forgot, will be a catalyst to the answers that you as individuals will find to your personal reality, to your world reality, and to your global reality.

Kathy Lester, **New Orleans Resources***, New Orleans*

With Love and Peace ...

Lazaris

Spiritual Growth

Love — Value — Higher Self & Negative Ego
Higher Self & Subconscious — The Power of Will
Growing through Joy — Processing & Programming
The Focuses of Life — Success & Its Secrets — The Success Cube
Our Aspiration — Humanity: The Next Step

Love

Q: For the person who picks up your book or some of your tapes, what would you say would be the first step? What would be your recommendation for someone who's just felt that gnawing, or who's just felt that need to explore? What's the best step?

Lazaris: The first step is to start with love. If you start with love and end with love, you can't go wrong. That's why the video tapes that we put together start with "Awakening the Love." There are no accidents.

How do you begin with love? You're expected to know. You're a grown-up, so you should know how to love. "You know how to love, don't you?" And everybody says, "Yes, of course, don't you?" Uncertainly, you answer, "Sure I do." Everybody says they know.

Nobody bothers to tell you how, and you are afraid to ask. Nobody bothers to take it apart for you. This is what you do, and this is what it produces, and this is how you go about it. We want to teach people how to learn to love themselves, then how to love others, then how to love their world. Always begin with love.

*Mary Pratt & Jack Clarke, **New Age Information Network**, Atlanta*

Q: Could you give us a very direct way of being love?

Lazaris: There are seven qualities and four levels that a person holds when they are enraptured, when they are enveloped either in the love that they are giving themselves or in the love that they are allowing themselves to receive from others, including the love received from God/Goddess/All That Is, or from their Higher Self.

First of all you feel a sense of security; you feel a sense of security in your life. Also you feel a sense of pleasure. That sense of pleasure (not just sexual pleasure, although not exclusive of it, either) includes all kinds of wonder, all kinds of warmth in your life.

As well as the security and pleasure, which form the foundation — level one — you also feel a sense of vulnerability: You are willing to expose your weaknesses. You are willing to expose to yourself and others where you are vulnerable, where you can be hurt. Then there is trust. The second level of "being love" is that feeling of vulnerability and that feeling of trust which includes being worthy of trust as well as being willing to trust.

"Love reduces all fears, save one: the fear of loss."

Beyond that a person who is being love is someone who is continuously reducing their fear of loss. The greatest fear that is associated with love is the fear of losing it.

Love reduces all fears, save one: the fear of loss. Indeed, if you have something that is worth $10.00, it's something that you might use, something that you might work with, something that you might not pay too much attention to. Then all of a sudden you find out: "No, no, no, it wasn't $10.00. It was $10,000.00!" Now you're going to treat this thing more dearly, more preciously, and be much more concerned if you were to lose it.

So it is with love: When it's frivolous and when it's silly, then you can toss it about and play with it, and not treat it with regard. But when suddenly it becomes valuable, when indeed it becomes deep, when you come to a place of needing, then its value increases, and you become terrified of losing it.

But there are ways even to reduce this fear of loss. In fact, when you love deeply enough, and are sure enough of the love that you have, when you openly communicate that love, then you can reduce the fear of loss. You can reduce the fear of loss by knowing that you are capable of loving and being loved, by knowing that you can *create* love. When you know you don't have to wait for love, but that you can engender it, that you can allow it to flow not only from you, but also to you, then you can reduce that fear of loss. It is a natural fear. It is so frequently associated with love. You can reduce it with the very thing that creates it: love. This is the third level of "being love."

Beyond that, there is the sense of being intimate and of being caring, and there is also the sense of knowing. You know, there are two ways you can know someone: You can know someone through pain, or you can know someone through love.

Studies have demonstrated that those who have been tortured as prisoners of war, and those who were in various concentration camps of World War II, developed a very strange and unique knowing relationship between the punisher and those who were punished.

You can know someone through pain. But a much healthier, a much more productive, a much more valuable method is through the loving. Intimacy, caring and knowing are the fourth level of "being love."

When you are in a place of being loved, when you are in a place of feeling that sense of *being* the very love, then you are in a place of feeling secure, of feeling pleasure, of feeling vulnerable and trusting, of having reduced your fear of loss because you know the love is emanating from within you, and you are filled with the feeling of intimacy (closeness and tenderness), of caring, and finally with a sense of knowing, knowing yourself, knowing your world, and knowing your relationships with those who are within both you and your world. Seven qualities, four levels of love.

Brian Williams, **Unicorn**, *Brisbane, Australia*

Value

Lazaris: So very much so. And so much of it has to do with the concept of value.

You know, not too long ago there was a horrible earthquake in Mexico City, and indeed there have been horrible hurricanes that have worked their way through the Gulf and even into the Southern portions of your own states — Louisiana and Mississippi. There was a hurricane (whatever name they gave it) that threatened Florida and the New Orleans area and that eventually hit in Mississippi, and it did devastating damage, including killing people.

A few weeks later there was another hurricane that moved up the East Coast and threatened Long Island and that area of the world. We said, at that time before it hit, that it would not cause any severe damage. We said the newscasters were blowing it way out of proportion, that it would not cause severe damage. When we were asked why, we responded that it was because individuals in and along the coastal regions from the Carolinas up through New York tend to value themselves more than a lot of the poor people in Mississippi, Louisiana and Mexico, who tend to devalue themselves. People on the East Coast, as a whole, value themselves, each other, and their property more than do people along the Gulf Coast, as a whole.

Therefore, we just have this image of the East Coast person standing out there and saying, "I dare you to take my property! I'll sue you!" There's that energy, that energy of value that says, "I deserve to have a better reality, and I will not stand for a reality that destroys me." In certain sections of your country people don't value themselves that much. In a sense, they have

Q: I have noticed that whatever endeavor others and I are involved with has a piece of that endeavor within me, within us. Often there is something that needs to be cleaned up through a gentleness, through a softness, through a forgiveness. What we have become involved in becomes something that is a part of us as well.

been taught and conditioned — erroneously! — to think that they are less valuable.

In other parts of your world you hear of Earthly destructions that kill so many thousands of people, in that sense. Those sorts of disasters, we'll tell you right off, cannot happen to that degree in your world because you value yourselves as individuals — you value yourselves more than many people in other places in the world. We are not saying there will be no disasters, nor are we saying there will be no death. No, we are not saying that.

As people value themselves, they create personally — in their personal accountability — a sphere of influence. That sphere has a radiance. It has a power to attract realities that are also valued and valuable. That sphere also has an energy that almost seems to repel realities that are less desirable — less valuable.

When you honestly value yourself, it is like walking around in a bubble of energy that operates in the metaphysical "like attracts like" fashion. Because you value yourself, you are empowered to create a valuable reality — a valuable world. When that value decreases, the bubble shrinks. When that value is all but gone, you seem to have no bubble at all.

Value is an attitude, that is for sure. But it's more than an attitude at the same time. Surround yourself in the bubble of value, and your reality and the world's reality will reflect that inherent and beautiful energy and essence.

It is not a perfect bubble, and the empowerment of value does not work perfectly, but as your value increases, so does the sphere of influence.

In other ways people will recognize that their world is a reflection of themselves, clearly so. The cancers in yourselves are the cancers in your world. The terrorists in your world reflect the martyrhood in your own being.

When terrorists refuse to let an airliner take off, how is your martyrhood impeding you in your attempts to take off, in your attempts to soar?

As you will be accountable for yourself, so you can be accountable for your world. As you value yourself, you will value your world, and improve its conditions.

A valuable future begins with a valuable you.

Murray Needleman, "The Murray Needleman Show," WWDB-Radio,
Philadelphia

Higher Self & Negative Ego

Lazaris: How do you distinguish between your Higher Self and your negative ego? That's where processing comes in.

This is a problem that's occuring in metaphysics now. Negative ego is an unpopular term. It's not fun to talk about. It's not popular. It doesn't draw audiences. And therefore, those who are in metaphysics to perform, those who are in metaphysics to draw large audiences, those who are doing it simply for the popularity don't want to talk about negative ego or ugly things like that. So therefore, they just chalk everything up to "the purposeful good. Everything happens for the purposeful good!" If you run into somebody or you get beat up or you get run over, well, that was for the purposeful good. ... {laughter} ... If you get fired, and if you get robbed — that's for the purposeful good. It's all for the purposeful good.

What is the purposeful good? The concept is put forth as though it is a truth about the way reality works. The connotation is that everything — "things" — by themselves and on their own always work out in

Q: How does one distinguish between the Higher Self speaking to you and the negative ego speaking to you?

the best way. With this connotation comes the implicit understanding that the good that is purposeful may take thousands upon thousands of years to reveal itself, but the good will eventually be there.

"Reality does not find its way Home; consciousness does. Reality does not work out for the purposeful good; consciousness works out for the purposeful good."

On one level this philosophy is correct. Eventually, the end result of all illusion — of all reality — is to become real — to return Home — and therefore eventually the purposeful good is achieved. This realization is of small comfort and of little value in the matrix of reality called here and now.

Additionally, it is important to make the distinction: What eventually results in the purposeful good, "things" or "consciousness"?

The reason everything eventually returns to the purposeful good is not a product of "things." It is a product of the consciousness. Because every "thing" has consciousness, it returns to the purposeful good, not just because it is a "thing."

Reality does not find its way Home; consciousness does. Reality does not work out for the purposeful good; consciousness works out for the purposeful good.

Now this may seem like an issue of semantics or like splitting philosophical hairs. But in your physical world, where so much communication relies on the vibration of words, very little is "just semantics," and it is important — sometimes critically important — to split philosophical hairs.

The important distinction is this: *If reality works for the purposeful good, then your involvement, your impact is not needed — it is superfluous. If consciousness works for the purposeful good, then your impact is more than desirable — it is essential.*

If reality works for the purposeful good, then your level of responsibility only affects the linear "speed" with which that good occurs. If consciousness works for the purposeful good, then your responsibility has an exponential impact not only on the speed, but also on the depth of good that will occur — the richness of that goodness.

If reality works for the purposeful good, then you can lull yourself into thinking and feeling that you don't really have to be responsible at all. After all, no matter how bad it gets, it will all work out for the purposeful good. This attitude, based upon a half-truth of metaphysics, is only fuel for the critics and detractors who suggest that the New Age fosters lethargy.

If consciousness works for the purposeful good, then that good will not occur until there is a change in consciousness. That change in consciousness occurs when beliefs and choices change. The purposeful good occurs when beliefs and choices evolve.

Each is responsible. Each is personally and socially responsible.

Hitler and Nazi Germany did not occur for the purposeful good. The events were not, nor ever will be, for the purposeful good. If Humanity would learn from those events, then the change of consciousness would be a purposeful good, but Humanity has not yet learned from those nightmarish events.

Further, whatever lessons you will eventually learn from Hitler and the Nazis could have been learned in a much more elegant way. This is a vitally important point: One needs to look not only at the potential purposeful good, one needs to look at the elegance of that good.

Whatever the lessons, they will not be worth the 6,000,000 Jews, the 12,000,000 Russians, and the countless millions of Allied soldiers who were killed. Whatever the lessons are that you will eventually learn — whatever that purposeful good is that eventually will

"No, Hitler and the Nazis were not part of a purposeful good. That atrocity was a global example of negative ego run rampant. It was an example of what can happen when you combine apathy and negative ego. It was an example of what happens when you stop caring and stop accepting responsibility."

be — it is not worth the multimillions of lives that were forever scarred or maimed by those events. There are statistics of the dead. What about the emotionally dead? Then one turns to the Pacific Theater, and the tragedy is amplified.

No, Hitler and the Nazis were not part of a purposeful good. That atrocity was a global example of negative ego run rampant. It was an example of what can happen when you combine apathy and negative ego. It was an example of what happens when you stop caring and stop accepting responsibility.

"If the subconscious is cluttered with negative ego, with self-importance, with delusions of grandeur, then what you're going to get, regardless of who says it, is delusions of grandeur, absolutely."

The *events* of that atrocity will never lead to a purposeful good. The *consciousness* in each of you can learn and change and eventually, if you will learn and heed the lessons, there will be a good that results.

That good will eventually be purposeful. It has not happened yet. When it does, the good that will come will not be a result of the reality. It will be the result of the consciousness. It will be a result of your consciousness.

When you do not want to deal with negative ego, it is easy to dismiss everything as a purposeful good. The half-truth can be more dangerous at times than no truth at all.

But everything gets chalked up that way, because you don't want to talk about negative ego.

As much as it is unpopular to deal with negative ego, it is inversely very popular to deal with your Higher Self. "Get in touch with your Higher Self." It is important to get in touch with your Higher Self — that it is. But if you avoid dealing with yourself, then it's dangerous to try to get in touch with your Higher Self, because you're going to find your negative ego instead.

We had a person who, on their own, got in touch with their Higher Self — short-cutted it. Their "Higher Self" told them that it — the "Higher Self" — had put a large amount of money in their bank account. The "Higher Self" told them: "Don't doubt us. Don't call the bank. Just go spend it."

And they did, and got into a lot of trouble. They wrote checks, lots of checks, and the checks all bounced, because there was no extra money in the bank. They attempted to bank on their negative ego. It never works!

There was another person we talked with. Well, we couldn't really talk with them. We listened to them as they told us ... {laughter} ... how their "Higher Self" told them to buy a house they couldn't afford. Their "Higher Self" said it would provide the money. They were told to go to Egypt where they would make miraculous discoveries that would save the world. They would be a hero — they would be praised world-wide. As we say, we couldn't talk to them, we could only listen. Fascinating! ... {laughter} ... It was their negative ego, totally and completely.

"Should I go to Egypt?" they asked us. We said, "Wait and see if your 'Higher Self' pays for the house first. ... {laughter} ... When your Higher Self doesn't pay for the house, don't go to Egypt." ... {laughter} ... Your negative ego can sound exactly like your Higher Self. It knows the jargon.

The first thing to understand is that you have a conscious self that is surrounded by a subconscious, and every bit of information that gets to you has to come through the subconscious. If the subconscious is cluttered with negative ego, with self-importance, with delusions of grandeur, then what you're going to get, regardless of who says it, is delusions of grandeur, absolutely.

Processing is when you clear out your negative ego. How do you know that your Higher Self is not your negative ego? Because you know your negative ego so well you know exactly what it says and how it says it. "Busting and Building Ego" is a tape we made for dealing with the negative ego. If you want to deal with it, deal with it. It works. You can bust that negative ego out of there.

You need to learn what your negative ego says, just as with a Vision Quest for Transmutation. First of all, you encounter your negative ego. What's its personality? What's its essence? What are its traits? Personify it. "So there, I know my negative ego. So when my Higher Self starts talking about how I'm better than everybody else and how I am really God's chosen one and no one realizes it, and because I'm so superior I get to do this and I get to do that, hey, that sounds exactly like my negative ego." Lo! It is.

Know your negative ego. That's how. Know what your negative ego sounds like. Process it. Bust your negative ego and replace it with a positive one. Clear out your payoffs. Clear out your game play. Handle your child. Put him or her in proper perspective. Handle your adolescent. Do the processing.

"The teacher is the one who helps you clear those stumbling blocks out of the way. The true teacher doesn't become one of those obstacles themselves."

Recognize, acknowledge, forgive and change. Ask yourself why. "Why is this? Why am I creating this? What are my beliefs? What are my attitudes? What are the thoughts and feelings? What are the choices and decisions? Why are they that way? What are my payoffs? What's my hidden agenda? What's my child doing? What's my adolescent up to? What's my negative ego up to? What's the parent part of me doing?"

Understand and know those parts and bust them out of there so that you clean up your subconscious. Then when you communicate with your Higher Self, and only then, do you have any semblance that it is your Higher Self.

Secondly, your Higher Self is going to have certain qualities about it. One: It's going to be consistent. Two: Its going to have its own identity. Three: It's going to be always expansive and loving. Four: It's never going to hurt you. It's never going to get in your way. It's never going to do it "for your own good."

Any teacher that says, "I stood in your way, I screwed you up, and I messed you up for your own good," is lying. Knowingly or unknowingly, they are not telling you the truth. We'll just put it that bluntly. Growth is intricate enough without being "helped" along by giving you more stumbling blocks. The teacher is the one who helps you clear those stumbling blocks out of the way. The true teacher doesn't become one of those obstacles themselves.

Some will tell you, "I had to get myself off the pedastal so I had to show you my dark side." You didn't have to have a dark side in the first place. The Higher Self doesn't have a dark side.

Also, there is one other thing we suggest whenever you work with counselors, whenever you work with your Higher Self: Do everything they tell you as long as it will not have a detrimental effect.

Because: Let's say you're communicating with your Higher Self, you think. You haven't done the steps. You see, we have come out with *The Sacred Journey: You and Your Higher Self*, a book which details, step-by-step, exactly what you do so that by the time you get there, there's no question whether this is your Higher Self or your negative ego. Of course it's your Higher Self. You know it is because you've prepared, because you've gotten there.

Let's say you think you're talking to your Higher Self, and it's really your negative ego, and it says, "Drive home on this route tonight." "Leave work 20 minutes later than normal." "Take a later flight." "Call up a friend — they need you desperately." "Move to Alaska by next Wednesday." "Your neighbor is trying to kill you, so kill them first." ... {laughter} ... "Quit your job." "They're out to get you because you know too much!" Or it says things like: "The Dark Forces are out to get you because you know too much." It's always amazing to us that it's the initiate, the novice in metaphysics, who "knows too much" that the Dark Forces are after. With people who've been involved with metaphysics for 20 years, 30 years, the Dark Forces are never after them! ... {laughter} ... If there were Dark Forces out to get you, they wouldn't have to look. ... {laughter} ... "I've got to keep running from the Dark Forces!" ... {laughter} ...

Of those things suggested, go ahead and take the different route home. Go ahead, wait 20 more minutes before you leave work. Go ahead, take the later flight. Don't take the one that you were planning to take. Go ahead, call the friend, because if you're wrong, there's no harm done. Don't quit your job. Don't move to Alaska. Don't kill your neighbor. ... {laughter} ... Because if you're wrong, you're in it deep! ... {laughter} ...

What will happen there is that if you follow the advice — even if it's your negative ego talking — your Higher Self will notice. Your Higher Self is always watching. It's there sort of watching over the edge of reality. It looks down and says, "Oh, look at that. Oh, my gosh, they're talking to their negative ego, and they think it's me! ... {laughter} ... Oh, well, they're not listening to it anyway, so it doesn't really matter, does it? ... {laughter} ... They're starting to listen to it! Well, we'd better do something about that!"

You see, you get all this information from your ego "Higher Self" and you don't act upon any of it. You just record it in the book for posterity. It's very funny.

It's always curious to us to hear of someone saying, "I've got a message from the extraterrestrials that has to get to the world." Why didn't they give it to George Schultz or somebody like that? ... {laughter} ... Henry Kissinger. These E.T.'s — they travel all these light years ... {laughter} ... with an important message to save the planet, and they're going to give it to ... {laughter} ... If they wanted to get into see George, they could. If they wanted to talk to Ronnie himself, they could. ... {laughter} ... They don't have to go through you who must martyr yourself. ... {laughter} ...

Consider: Your own negative ego may be playing one horrendous joke on you! ... {laughter} ... "I'M AN E.T. (snicker, snicker, snicker) ... {laughter} ... I'VE BEEN SENT HERE BY THE COUNCIL OF COUNCILS, AND YOU HAVE BEEN CHOSEN AS OUR EMISSARY TO BRING PEACE (snicker, snicker) TO THE WORLD! ... {laughter} ... YOU MUST ORGANIZE 45 COUNCILS ... {laughter} ... AND YOU MUST LEAD THEM ALL! ... {laughter} ... AND I WILL TELL YOU WHAT TO DO." ... {laughter} ...

Well, if you don't listen to any of that stuff, your Higher Self isn't going to interfere. We're not saying listen to *that* stuff, but in that sense, take the harmless information and act on it, because if you do the harmless things and nothing comes of it, then you're either going to bust your own ego, or your Higher Self is somehow going to interfere and say, "Look, we can't let you keep this up." So that's a way to tell the difference.

But see, this is why processing is so important. People don't want to process. "Do I have to get in touch with my feelings?" Yes.

"Do I have to think?" Yes.

"Do I have to figure out what my child and my adolescent ..." Yes! You do!

"Well, if I create my own reality, can't I create it another way?" No, because those are the rules you wrote!

You created this whole reality to give yourself that opportunity. Don't get cold feet. Go ahead and do what you came here to do, which is to figure out how you do create your reality consciously and to have fun doing it!

Some who claim to teach will take the simpler and more popular stance and tell you that you don't need to process or program your reality. They will offer any number of simple and often ineffective non-truths or half-truths. Sometimes the techniques will work, which is a credit to your willingness and determination, not the efficiency or effectiveness of the technique. In the short term what they offer is more convenient and streamlined. Instant metaphysics and spirituality. Experiment if you like.

You do a tremendous disservice to yourself. But then, when you figure it out they're not going to be anywhere around to talk to. They're not going to be around. You won't be able to get hold of them. "Hey, you told me this, and it wasn't true!" You'll get a letter back stamped: "You create your own reality, sucker. Why'd you do it?"

Well, we don't sense that is a fair answer, either. Although it's not popular, we continuously talk of the importance of processing, and programming — not just programming, not just processing, but the combination of the two as the one-two punch to create the reality.

Higher Self & Subconscious

Lazaris: Worlds of difference. Worlds of difference. Your subconscious is like a pet, something there to please you, whichever "you" you want to be pleased. The Higher Consciousness is much more.

Q: What's the difference between your subconscious and your Higher Self?

We divide it this way: Your conscious mind is in charge of your conscious reality. Power is conscious. It is in charge of the *context* and the *form*. It is also in charge of the *content*. Your conscious mind is in charge of your conscious world totally and completely. The subconscious mind handles the *content* of your *inner* worlds. You still handle the *context* and the *form*. The content of your inner worlds, contained within your subconscious mind, must become conscious to be useful. As it's brought to the surface, you determine what *context* it's going to be placed in — what the backdrop is — and you determine what *form* it will take — how that communication is going to come to you.

Your unconscious mind contains all the data dealing with your *other* worlds. Subconscious is inner, unconscious is other world (between lifetimes, past, present, future, parallel, overlapping). It contains the *content*, but consciously you still hold the *form* and the *context* in which that information is presented. The *content* is in the unconscious, but the *form* and the *context* is in the conscious mind.

The Higher Conscious Mind contains all the information regarding all your growth, your evolution, and your enlightenment, which therefore includes the other minds, absolutely. It contains all the data — the *content* — regarding your enlightenment and your growth, but you, consciously, still hold the *context* and the *form*.

That's why we say don't share the *context* and the *form* of a meditation because that's yours. The content can come from your conscious, your subconscious, your unconscious, or your Higher Conscious mind, but the form and the context are always yours, and that's why it's really meaningless to anybody else. The content may be of interest and may even be helpful, but the *context* and *form* are yours.

So what is the difference between your subconscious mind and your Higher Consciousness? Your subconscious is but a gathering place of data to provide for and protect the conscious world, and to provide for and protect the inner world reality. The Higher Conscious includes the subconscious, and it is much, much more. It holds the answers to and the love for your spirituality, your enlightenment, and your growth.

Q: With all the things that I have to do in my life, should Spirituality really be number one?

Lazaris: Yes. Unequivocally yes. Because, you see, all those other things you do in your life *are* your spirituality. We talk about politics. We talk about economics. We talk about sociology. We talk about psychology.

We talk about all these things, because they're all part of your spirituality, because your spirituality is your relationship with God/Goddess/All That Is. Everything in your reality is a part of God/Goddess/All That Is. Therefore, your work should be approached spiritually — your play, your obligations, your bill paying, your economic decision-making, your social life, your intimate life. Everything is a part of your spirituality. In fact, your spirituality *is* number one.

There really hasn't been a war fought that didn't involve relationships with God/Goddess/All That Is. Every act of violence is somehow connected. Every conflict is a fight over or about that energy. Everything you do positively and lovingly is obviously somehow related to God/Goddess/All That Is. And since Spirituality is your relationship, thus it is so.

It is number one. Yours is to come to peace with that, and to get into harmony with that without having to sacrifice anything except your martyrhood, your negative ego, your manipulations and your game play.

Accept it. Work with developing it so that you can be at peace with that truth.

Anonymous Question, Evening with Lazaris, Atlanta, 1987

The Power of Will

Lazaris: Will or will power ... Actually, the terms have two different meanings, quite clearly. We suggest that will power, on the positive side, can be a sense of great determination, and on the negative side can be a great stubbornness. Whichever it is, determination or stubbornness, positive or negative, it always involves a certain degree of struggle.

Q: Will you define "will" or "will power"?

In your world, struggle has been, unfortunately, nobilized. People value will power whether it's negative (stubborn, bull-headed, struggling with that stubbornness, or struggling with bullheadedness), or even if it's positive (struggling with their determination, struggling with the implementation of that determination). Will power involves, as a common denominator, struggle. It also involves, as a common denominator, the exertion of force.

By reversing the words you have the "power of will." The words sound very similar on the surface and sound as if they represent only a semantic difference. However, it is quite different terminology altogether. The power of will has nothing to do with force, nor with struggle.

The power of will is a power of letting, letting it be — not "making it be" or "having it be" or "insisting that it be." Letting it be.

Each person has within them a will, a will that includes their destiny — what they have come to do in this lifetime. A true destiny is always self-chosen.

You have a will that includes a sense of remembering Home, remembering your relationship with God/Goddess/All That Is ... remembering that original place to which you are trying to return. There is a will within each person, and that will has a tremendous amount of power.

When a person is willing to accept their destiny by choosing it, willing to understand their focuses by exploring them, willing to open themselves to their vision by imagining it, and willing to let themselves remember their relationship with God/Goddess/All That Is by feeling it, they have a tremendous power within them ... a power that generates miracles.

The power of the will is the power that can generate your reality the way you want it to be. With it, you can experience dominion in your reality; that is, you can deal with a world that is dealing with you on friendly terms, where you are co-creating your reality out of the joy and the celebration of life rather than out of the need to struggle.

When you use the power of will, you let the obstacles move out of the way and allow yourself to move gracefully, with elegance, and with excellence, through your life. That, perhaps, is the best way to describe the difference between the elegance of the power of will and the struggle of will power.

Lazaris: Anything that you can see, taste, touch, hear or smell is the illusion. It is the illusion of tangibility. But when you touch something, the gentleness and the softness, the comfort, the safety, the wonderfulness that you emotionally feel are what is real. Similarly, with whatever you see, it is meaningless unless there is a feeling attached to it.

Q: Will you define the emotions that we experience and the relationship or importance of those emotions in the physical existence?

That is why we say the tangibility of the five senses is the illusion. The reality is the emotion sparked by that illusion. So we suggest, first of all, that the emotions that you feel are what's real in your reality. You have a broad and an expansive reality, absolutely, and it is mostly created as a "trick of light," as it might be called.

Your reality is a trick of light and mirrors. It is like a hologram — a holographic image. The only thing that allows the illusion to be real is the emotion that lies beneath it.

Your society generally divides emotions into two categories: those that are considered positive and those that are considered negative. The meaning that most people attach to the division is that the positive emotions are clearly such things as love, joy, happiness, laughter, safety, wonder and curiosity, although some feelings cross over. After all, there is the phrase, "Curiosity killed the cat."

Then there are the "negative emotions," of course, and anger and hurt are two of perhaps the most common, in that sense. There's a range of emotion that includes anxiety, fear, worry, doubt, confusion and various others that are considered negative. Calling these emotions negative is something of a misnomer, a misnomer that has caused a tremendous amount of pain for people.

"... what a negative emotion really is, is any emotion that is denied. A positive emotion is any emotion that is honestly expressed."

What has happened is that you have learned that you should not feel "negative emotions." You learn that you should only feel positive emotions. In your attempts to shortcut your growth, you have tried to alleviate your anger, hurt, fears, etc., by suppressing them, by forgetting them, by refusing to believe that you feel them. Therefore, the angers that you have get suppressed, depressed and internalized, and ultimately they show up as illness. They can show up as cancer or show up as various other kinds of illnesses that you "die from."

We would point out that what a negative emotion really is, is any emotion that is denied. A positive emotion is any emotion that is honestly expressed. If you feel love, but will not admit it, and pretend it's not true, you may develop heart difficulty, most definitely so. Complications and problems of the heart can develop because a traditionally positive emotion — love — has become negative because you won't express it, because you won't deal with it. You won't admit it. You won't allow yourself to feel love.

Similarly, if you have anger, and you express it and talk about it, or write it out, or meditate it out with the intention of releasing it, then your anger is the most positive feeling you've got. Anger can be very positive when expressed appropriately.

Therefore, if you will express any number of those feelings that are traditionally negative, they are no longer negative. They become positive because they're expressed, they're out, and you can let go of them.

As you can express your love, joy, happiness, and celebration, in that way, those become very positive as well, because you can express them and grow from them. If you refuse to express any emotion, if you deny that you feel it, you are turning whatever it is into a negative emotion.

As regards human relationships, you've created yourself, and you've created your playground, and you also have created all these other people. That wasn't just because you were lonely. It was because you wanted to interact, to relate, to reach out and touch. You wanted someone else to reach out and touch you back. Therefore, you wanted to create a world in which there were people with whom to interact. You created this phenomenon called relationship.

From the very simplest of relationships (i.e., from the impact that you experience at seeing that there's another person on your planet — that you're not alone) to the ultimate relationship (i.e., deep intimacy in a loving relationship) the whole gamut of emotion is available. In the simplest of relationships (I see you and you see me at a distance, and we realize we're not alone), there is the full range of emotion from total love to total hate. In the most loving relationship (where we are intimate, working and functioning as one), there is the full range of emotion from total love to total hate — because emotions are real. Now admittedly, most people won't experience the gamut of emotion, but it's important to realize that the availability, the potential, is there.

"If you refuse to express any emotion, if you deny that you feel it, you are turning whatever it is into a negative emotion."

Patricia Clay, **Infinite Thought**, San Diego

Growing through Joy

Q: You have
said the
planet, like
any conscious-
ness, does not
need to grow
through pain,
that "pain is
not the only
way." How
can planet
Earth grow
and evolve in
a way other
than up-
heaval and
destruction?
How can it
shift into
higher levels
of conscious-
ness more
smoothly, and
how can we
help?

Lazaris: Everyone talks about the New Age. Some say it's coming. Others say it's already here. While they all talk of the New Age, no one really stops to look at what the Old Age was about. We suggest the Old Age method is one that involves struggle and hardship. The Old Age attitude says, "If something is worth having, it's worth struggling over, waiting for." It nobilizes all these sorts of puritanical concepts. It proposes that you should work hard all your life, and then when you are old and can't work any longer, you can enjoy your life.

Initially, you were never supposed to struggle. You were never supposed to suffer. You were never supposed to have pain in the creating of this playground that is your Earth. The creating of this illusion that is the physical plane of reality was never supposed to be hard. It was meant to be a joyous, celebratory experience of growing.

We will use a bit of an analogy here to describe where pain began. As you tripped along as consciousnesses, playing the roles of the gods you are, somebody stubbed their toe and it hurt. Rather than saying, "I goofed," they said, "Oh no, I intended to do that. I planned to stub my toe, to inflict pain upon myself."

Why? "Because it purifies me." Yes, that's it! That sounds real good. "I stubbed my toe and it really hurts, but there was a benefit, you see — it really made me grow, and therefore, I'm more advanced than you. In fact, if you had any sense at all, you'd be wise like me and go out and stub your toe, too."

If I can convince enough of you to do it, then I have been vindicated from my mistake, and it somehow becomes a virtue.

You can grow through struggle. Your adversity can be a motivator to end adversity. Your pain can be a motivator to stop the pain.

All of Eastern religion and Western thought have been built upon this concept of struggling. The new method of growth is to grow through joy and love — to see life not as something you have to confront and win over, but something to encounter and celebrate. You can learn through the pain, but you can learn so much more rapidly through the joy of life.

Another false myth is that you need to experience pain to appreciate love and happiness. We liken this limiting belief to an analogy of when you were a little child, and you had your first bite of ice cream. You immediately knew, "Hey, this is good!!" You didn't need to drink sour milk first to know that the sweet taste of ice cream was delightful.

Likewise, you do not need to struggle to appreciate the value of a struggle-free life. The human consciousness is evolved enough, and people are sophisticated enough to recognize the value of love and joy. It is time to drop the struggle, to drop the suffering and appreciate it for what it was. Don't make yourself wrong or beat yourself up, but realize that it is time for you as an individual to let go of the Old Age and enter a New Age. Grow by these more joyous methods.

What we have been doing these many years of working with people is consistently showing them techniques to help them grow through the happiness, the laughter, and the wonder of it all. Thousands of people whom we have worked with are indeed discovering just that. They are continuously creating even more love, more happiness, and more success in their lives through the "wonderfulness" of who they are, rather than following the suffering, struggling, hardship routes they were taught in other lifetimes, as well as in the earlier portion of this one.

It is time for a new way, a New Age of growing. And the most important point is that it works.

Paul Zuromski, **Body, Mind & Spirit**, Johnston, Rhode Island

Q: Humanity has chosen to learn and grow through suffering. It seems now that more people are gradually awakening to the possibility of learning through joy. What suggestions do you have for people who want to strengthen that possibility, that ability, to learn through joy?

Lazaris: Most definitely, we would suggest it is encouraging — your observation is quite correct. Suffering, struggling and being in pain have been, so-to-speak, the "fare" of growth, what it has always been. Many have seen struggle as the only way of evolving. They felt there was no other way to grow. We, in that sense, were one of the first to most clearly and most specifically talk of joy and happiness. We still surprise many people with even the contemplation of such as an avenue of growth. Therefore, as more and more are coming upon that understanding and opening up to that possibility, we are very gratified and very pleased.

How can one move in that direction more completely and more fully to start growing though joy? The first step — the vital step — is to recognize how much you want to believe that pain is the only way of growth. You need to be willing to establish a foundation. For all the years of pain, for all the time devoted to struggle, you need to realize: "I wanted it that way." Or, "I thought it was the only way. I felt it was the only way."

You need to be honest. "Everyone said it was the only way, and I didn't bother looking any deeper." You really need to look at and to recognize that you wanted the pain as the only way of growth for varying reasons. You really need to acknowledge: it was you who wanted it. Surely you may have been taught. Surely you may have been shown by demonstration, and in that sense, various people who put themselves up as leaders, as gurus, as masters may have instructed you: "No pain, no gain."

"You can still grow through pain if you desire. It's not as though that avenue is shut to you, but a new avenue is open to you."

However, you need to look deeper and to recognize that you create your own reality, and therefore you created being taught and being told that pain was the only avenue of growth that was available. As you can recognize that, as you can acknowledge that, then you can forgive yourself, forgive yourself for having bought the lie, and forgive yourself for having believed the limitations, forgive yourself for having been caught up in what is truly the Old Age and the old sense of growth that has been so predominant in your world.

Then, we suggest, the change can occur. You can open your hearts and open your heads — both, in that particular regard — to the possibility that you can grow through joy, that there is an alternative.

You can still grow through pain if you desire. It's not as though that avenue is shut to you, but a new avenue is open to you. Therefore, recognize, acknowledge, forgive and change. This process can move you very powerfully and very beautifully forward — forward with love, light, laughter, and joy.

Secondly, look at the belief, and literally change the belief. Understand that all beliefs are illusion, and therefore pick those illusionary beliefs that work most effectively for you. What advantage do you get from believing in the fear and in the pain? What alternative advantages might you receive by believing in the joy and in the laughter?

We realize some say you can't "try" anything. We suggest, well, go ahead and try it anyway! Go ahead and call it what you will, but let yourself try, and see what happens as you go for the joy, as you go for the laughter, as you go for the wonder of what your reality is. This is the third step: Try joy!

As you try it and find out it works, that is the grandest impetus for the continuation, which is the fourth component. Once you begin the joy, once you begin the laughter, and discover the beauty of it, let yourself lighten up, etc. Realize that maybe you were foolish for taking life so seriously and so heavily before, but to continue that foolishness does not eliminate it. Therefore, be willing to admit, "All right. I found a new way." Rather than feeling guilty, or letting pride get in the way, let yourself unabashedly rush forward into that new way of growing, through the joy and the laughter, and let yourself lightly continue.

It was Alan Watts who said, "Angels fly because they take themselves lightly." We suggest that that is a rather profound statement. Take these four steps, and let yourself fly.

*Van Ault, **Magical Blend**, San Francisco*

Processing & Programming

L azaris: At first it looks like a contradiction, but eventually it's not. "Trust the process?" What process? You'd better know what process you're supposed to be trusting. The phrase "trust the process" sounds good, but do you know what it means? If you do, and the process that you're trusting is a good process, then trust it, certainly so.

Q: You've talked about processing and programming and changing the blueprint. You hear a lot about allowing your Higher Self to direct. "Let go and let God." "Trust the process." Do those phrases fit in?

We recommend that you "trust the process of processing," "trust the process of programming," "trust the process of doing what you're on this Physical Plane to do," and that is to learn to have fun and to consciously create success. If that's your process, then by all means trust it.

Trust your Higher Self? Definitely so, BUT ...

Let us put it this way: "Trust what you see." But what if you're blind? "Trust everything you hear." But what if you're deaf? What if there's so much sand and so much fuzz in front of you that you can't see much of anything, other than abstract shapes and forms? What if there's too much noise — the rock music is playing so loud. "What? I couldn't hear you." See, that's what we're talking about.

Process and program to clear your eyes so you can see. Clear your ears so you can hear. Clean out the subconscious garbage that you carry so that you can hear what your Higher Self is saying. This is how it fits together, and this is where we would suggest many as yourselves get confused.

You're told pieces of truth, but not the whole of the truth, and then you end up going around in circles wondering why your life's not working. It's not because what you're told isn't true, but because what you are told isn't *fully* true.

We're going to draw a bit of a mental schematic here, a very large circle, and it's very rough. Here's your Higher Self, as a broad representation of everything that is. Inside the circle is you. That dot is this physical lifetime, and all those other dots are your other lifetimes, all of them out here, all of the lifetimes. Here's a group in Atlantis, and here's some in Lemuria, and here's some in Egypt, and these dots — your lifetimes — are all over the place. And this little one right here, that one's you! Around this conscious self you have a subconscious mind. And we like to draw that subconscious like little fuzz, little sticky antennae, because what it does is gather every bit of information that comes into your concept, into your life.

Tell us, for example, every license plate you've ever seen from the State of Texas in numerical and alphabetical order. You can't do that. Your subconscious could. In hypnosis, you could list out every Texas license plate you have ever seen.

Tell us the prices of everything on the menu of the restaurant you ate in last Thursday — or the last restaurant you ate in over six months ago. Your subconscious has all that information. It's stored there. It's useless to you, and so your subconscious doesn't let it through to your conscious mind.

However, your subconscious also contains all the junk, all the limited beliefs that you hold, all the ideas that your adolescent picked up, all the misconceptions of the child and all the screwy, idiotic ideas that the world has put out there — your subconscious has them.

Now out here is your Higher Self, and it sends a message directly to you. What does it have to go through? Your subconscious mind. Now, if your subconscious mind is filled with a lot of clutter, what's going to happen to the message from your Higher Self? It's going to get cluttered. Therefore, just like static on Radio Free Europe, you're not going to hear it, or what you hear may not be your Higher Self at all, but may be your negative ego, or some cockamamie idea that you heard from some screwball on the radio or on television. It may be from some television movie that you fell asleep to, and therefore you drank in all that information.

Have you ever listened to the lyrics that your subconscious is reading? "Love is painful. Love is hurtful. Love is terrible. I can't live without it. I can't live with it. It's awful. It's disgusting. I don't know how I can deal with it. You broke my heart. You broke my heart. I'm blue, I'm blue, I'm terribly blue."

All of that is in there. All those messages about love are in there, and you wonder why relationships don't work! They don't work because you've got all that clutter. Do you hear the words? Do you hear some of the words that you listen to? You fall asleep, and you're watching television. All those suggestions, all those programmings are going in there, absolutely. Every horror movie you've seen, every blood-and-guts slasher movie you've ever watched, is in your subconscious mind, and you wonder why you create fear in your reality out here. You wonder why you do those sorts of things. Because it's there!

All right, now you tell us what kind of clarity you're going to get when you just trust your Higher Consciousness before you've cleared out all the stuff. You're going to get a lot of gobbledygook. You're going to get school teachers and Sunday school teachers telling you: "You'll never amount to anything. You'll never accomplish anything. You need to have pain in order to grow. You need to suffer in order to really value some-

"We actually had a person tell us once that they got in touch with their Higher Self, and their Higher Self was kicking them in the stomach. And we just said, 'Don't insult your Higher Self like that. If you are going to be that destructive to yourself, do it, but don't blame your Higher Self. Don't lay that one on your Higher Self'."

thing." You can have all that gunk, and your "Higher Self" is going to start telling you that sort of thing.

We actually had a person tell us once that they got in touch with their Higher Self, and their Higher Self was kicking them in the stomach. And we just said, "Don't insult your Higher Self like that. If you are going to be that destructive to yourself, do it, but don't blame your Higher Self. Don't lay that one on your Higher Self. Your Higher Self would never kick you in the stomach. Your Higher Self would never treat you badly. Your Higher Self would never teach you a lesson the hard way. That's your garbage — not your Higher Self's."

You see, when you have that kind of garbage in your subconscious, it will clutter Higher Self communication. Perhaps you had a third-grade teacher who tricked you and forced you into learning the hard way. Now your Higher Self talks like that. No, it doesn't! Your third-grade teacher talks like that — not your Higher Self!

When you've got the gunk, the garbage, in your subconscious, it is going to produce garbage in your communications. Even if it is your actual Higher Self communicating, the information can be garbled or wrong because it's got to come through the subconscious to get to you.

That's why you begin by your processing, and when you have cleared your subconscious, which many people have, then absolutely listen to the will of your Higher Self. Let your Higher Self guide you. Let it direct you and lead you in that way. Absolutely so!

You see, that's what we're working toward. You can't run until you learn how to walk, and far too many people, in that sense, want to run. It's beautiful that you want to run. But don't hate yourself so much that you refuse to learn how to walk first.

You see, we talk of processing and programming, and someone comes along and says, "Don't do that. Just trust God. Let go and let God." Catchy phrase, almost lyrical. But what does it mean? What is "God" going to tell you? What kind of God do you have?

What kind of God do you have? If you're a Catholic, you've got a pretty difficult one. If you're Jewish, you have a totally different kind of God. If you're Baptist, your God says, "Don't dance. Don't smoke. Don't drink. Don't have fun. Don't wear makeup. Wear plain clothes." If you're a Free Methodist, look as drab as you can. If you're a Methodist, your God says, "Hey, have a good time!"

The "Gods" that you have are different, but not because God is different, but because your subconscious reads that information. Even what we are saying to you now is filtering through your subconscious, and if your subconscious is filled with all kinds of mother/father junk, then you're going to project father onto us and either try to make us into a father that will take care of you, or make us into a father that you have to rebel against. But it's your stuff, not ours. And it's your stuff, not God's — your stuff, not your Higher Self's.

Therefore, "let go and let God" when you are clear enough to let go and let God. Let your Higher Self guide you when you are clear enough to allow your Higher Self to guide you — when you are ready, when you are ready. Until you love yourself totally, work on clearing the stuff out.

"The 'Gods' that you have are different, but not because God is different, but because your subconscious reads that information."

You might want to look at why you're so eager to skip this one. Why? What are you afraid you're going to find? What's so awful about processing that you don't want to do it? What's so awful about programming that you want to skip that step and turn it all over to your Higher Self? Why do you hate yourself so much that you're going to deprive yourself of one of the most beautiful opportunities you have?

Why do you hate yourself so much that you're going to abnegate all that you've created this physical reality for (to learn to have fun, to learn to consciously create success)? Why put that all together and then turn your back on it? You need to love yourself more. You need to respect yourself more. You need to care for yourself. And yes, move toward "letting God." Move toward "letting your Higher Self." But clear out the junk on the way.

We work with many, many people who are there. They have processed, and we now say, "All right, let's get there. Let's do that. Let's just let your Higher Self work with it. Turn this one over to your Higher Self." Those of you who have been involved in our workshops on the Causal Plane and who are dealing with your Higher Self know that you are already doing that — turning over many of the problems, many of the issues to your Higher Self. But you get to that. Love yourself enough...

Anonymous Question, Evening with Lazaris, Seattle, 1987

The Focuses of Life

Lazaris: Well, indeed at first it does sound too simple. Perhaps all great truths sound initially as though they're almost too simple to be true, and you're right in the sense that people want to think and to look for a great deal more complication in life.

When you take it apart — to learn to have fun — the first emphasis is on the learning, not just on having fun, not just showing up at the right parties and knowing the right people, but actually *learning* to have fun — learning to be the originator, to be the source, of fun.

To that end, the word fun itself, here, continuously is expanding and changing. Therefore, what was fun for you in your 20s now you reevaluate in your 30s and you have quite different opinions. Hopefully, you intend that by the time you are in your 40s and 50s and 60s, etc., that you will have yet even different and perhaps more profound definitions of this word.

To learn to have fun is not a "To Do" item that can be easily checked off the list, but rather is something that you are continuously and expressively working with throughout your life.

Similarly, with learning to consciously create success, again the emphasis is on the learning — not just being successful — not just being born to the right family, going to the right school, getting the right job and knowing how to polish the right apples. It means learning how to create the reality consciously whereby you are successful — and continuously, again, working with that definition of success.

The teenager in each person has certain ideas of what success is in terms of the accomplishments of an even-

Q: You often say that human beings are here on Earth to have fun and to learn to consciously create success.

Lazaris: Exactly.

Q: That sounds too simple.

ing or a weekend, but as you grow older and wiser and become more aware and more alert, those definitions become much more intricate, much more involved. Thus the learning becomes not more difficult, but more intricate. Therefore, again, it is an ongoing activity along these lines.

*"When sim-
plicity replaces
intricacy and
accuracy, your
metaphysics be-
comes plati-
tudinously
filled with 'al-
ways's' and
'never's'. Your
spirituality be-
comes riddled
with dogma.
That's what
happened to
the traditional
spirituality.
Don't let it hap-
pen to the New
Spirituality."*

Further, perhaps the statement sounds somewhat simplistic, and we suggest here that that can be, sometimes, the trap, because it sounds far too easy, and therefore gets overlooked for a far more illusionary and struggling reality creation. In fact, very few consciously know how to create success, and very few know how to have fun.

Just witness your world around you with all its anger and all its hurt and all its misery. The vast majority of those upon your planet have yet to learn these two things, and you've been at it for several hundreds of thousands of years. Maybe it sounds easy, but it certainly hasn't been proving to be.

So many confuse intricacy and difficulty. Reality is intricate. You made it that way. That it is intricate, however, does not mean it has to be difficult. No one wants life to be difficult. We have continuously suggested that life was never meant to be difficult. Life is meant to be easy. We have encouraged you to always live with ease.

Many, in their search for ease, not only attempt to reduce the difficulty; they also eliminate the intricacy. Some leaders advocate the simplicity above all. They advocate simplicity above intricacy and, more sadly, they emphasize simplicity above accuracy.

When simplicity replaces intricacy and accuracy, your metaphysics becomes platitudinously filled with "always's" and "never's". Your spirituality becomes riddled with dogma. That's what happened to the traditional spirituality. Don't let it happen to the New Spirituality.

Lazaris: To change? Maybe the term more appropriate to use would be "to expand," absolutely. When one learns to have fun, and reaches certain levels of that fun, and learns to create certain levels of success, admittedly so, there is the desire to seek and stretch and reach for more. It is not in a greedy way. It is rather a sense of curiosity. It is not in a sense of possessiveness, but in a sense of celebration — to have more fun and to have more success.

Yes, once you've reached those levels of accomplishment through the physicality, you don't leave it behind you, by any means. You expand beyond it so as to learn to have fun and to create success on yet higher, more intricate levels of evolution. Therefore, these two focuses, as we call them, these two reasons for being, not only apply to those of you who have chosen to demonstrate yourselves in a physical manner, but also apply to all growing consciousnesses. From the simplest cell to the most intricate of cellular structures, to beyond that which is cellular, into the energy levels of consciousness, there is the desire to learn to have fun, and to learn to consciously create success.

Yes, it does involve transforming — it involves expanding your physical, mental, emotional and intuitive selves. Ultimately, the fun and success mean reaching and finding your Future Self, and then your Higher Self. Learning to have fun will eventually mean reaching and touching God/Goddess/All That Is.

Q: If anyone were actually able to accomplish those two objectives, wouldn't that require them to go through total transformation — not just more human goodness, but to change on a deep spiritual level as well, to change mentally, psychologically, psychically?

*Van Ault, **Magical Blend**, San Francisco*

Q: What is the purpose of life? There seem to be so many answers to this question. What's the bottom line? Why are we here really?

Lazaris: "What is the purpose of life? ... What is my task? Why am I here? ... Why am I physical? What is my mission?"

You are haunted by this desire to know. Deep within your brain stirs the thought that if you just knew the answer to one of these questions, then everything else would make sense. Your heart echoes with feelings that a satisfactory answer would make everything ... absolutely everything ... all right.

Your purpose, your mission, your task — or, as we prefer to say, your focus — can be stated with disarming ease. The prime reason you are here: To learn to have fun.

Yes. That's it. You are here to learn to have fun! You have created a physical form and a physical world to put it in. You have created all of your reality to give yourself the opportunity to learn — to learn to have fun.

The critics and detractors pounce upon that statement as proof of the shallowness and hedonism of the New Age. They either get angry at the apparent lack of social responsibility, or they dismiss the idea as the empty-headed "fad philosophy" of this yuppie "sport" called the New Age.

Many who consider themselves part of the alternative spirituality of the New Age want the purpose, the task, the mission to be more serious or to at least sound more spiritual. Missions should be loftier. A purpose of connecting with your Higher Self or becoming one with the Source sounds much more reasonable. It sounds much more valuable and viable.

At first glance, these criticisms seem to have merit. Upon further investigation the kind of fun we are talking about, the kind of fun you are attempting to learn, is valuable and totally viable. We are talking about the kind of fun derived from accomplishing the lessons you have selected to experience and fulfilling the destinies you have chosen to explore. Your spiritual focus — your spirituality — is all about your living, breathing, loving embracing relationship with God/Goddess/All That Is. This is what learning to have fun is all about.

Your purpose, mission, task — your focus — is not only about achievement; it is also about the means of achieving. It is not just about succeeding — it is also about the way in which you succeed. You can grow through the struggles and hardships of life. Some of you needed to do that. Some still feel the need to struggle and suffer. However, you also have the choice to grow through the love and the laughter.

Which is going to be more fun? Both of them will "get you there," but which is going to be more fun? Everyone, regardless of their spirituality or their claimed lack of it, has the same purpose, task, mission, the same focus: Learning to have fun.

Certainly the desire to reach a heaven, whether it is a literal place or a state of mind, is a desire to have fun. Certainly a desire to connect with your Higher Self or with the Source is a desire to have fun — a postponed desire perhaps, but still a desire to have fun. For the Christian, certainly being on the right side of the rapture is a goal of having fun. No matter how much struggle you think is required — no matter how painful the path you decide you must have, the goal, the culmination of your learning, is to reach a state of peace. Peace. That's fun!

There are four keys to understanding this primary focus.

First, learn. The focus is not just "to have fun" — it's to learn. It is: To learn to have fun. Learning means recognizing and acknowledging that you are the creator of all the possibilities, probabilities, and actualities of your

"Your spiritual focus — your spirituality — is all about your living, breathing, loving embracing relationship with God/Goddess/All That Is. This is what learning to have fun is all about."

reality. It involves figuring out what you did "right" and "wrong." Learning to have fun means being responsible for what "works" in your life. It means figuring out the "why's" and the "how's" of reality creation so that the fun you have is the fun you know you created. It is self-generated fun. You never have to wonder if it will last, because you create it — you are the source of the fun, then the happiness, and finally the joy you are having in your life.

"Fun is not static. Being fluid, it always changes."

Second, define. Define fun continuously. Fun is not static. Being fluid, it always changes. When you were six, you had very distinct ideas of what a fun day was all about. Now those same ideas would seem ridiculous! Your current concepts of fun are unique. As you unfold your future, your current pictures of fun will also change. It is vital that you define and redefine what you mean by "fun" and what you mean by having it.

Third, balance. Despite the parental "tape-loops" inside your head mumbling something about beds that you must sleep in and cakes you cannot eat, it is important to balance. It is up to you to choose and decide not only what's fun, but when it's fun. For some, a "pizza and a six-pack" may not only sound like a fun idea — at the time, it just might be the essence of fun! Yet, at another time it would be the antithesis. It is up to you to balance the long-term fun and the short-term pleasures. It is up to you to distinguish among the inner-child's, adolescent's, young-adult's, and the spiritual adult's sense of: "What is fun?"

Learning to have fun is not just about being at the right place at the right time, knowing where the best parties are on a Friday night, or about knowing the right people. It is about learning, defining, and balancing self-generated fun. It is about creating your own reality and being positively responsible for that creation.

Fourth, deserve. The final key to understanding the prime focus of having fun is also the major blockage to its fulfillment.

You can learn, define, and even balance what is fun for you. You can process and program. You can work with a myriad of techniques. You can be responsible and enjoy the power implicit within that responsibility. You can learn and work through the psychological and metaphysical obstacles that separate you from the reality you ask for.

However, if you don't think you deserve, all of the above are intellectual exercises fast becoming exercises in frustration and futility. The lack of deserving permeates your beliefs and attitudes, your thoughts and feelings, and your choices and decisions. You do not feel you deserve. A primary focus that seems easy enough to accomplish has just been moved out of reach. Because it is beyond your belief and therefore your choice, "you can't get there from here."

There are several powerful reasons that deserving is outside the belief-choice matrix.

1. You were taught. You were taught by parents, teachers, spiritual leaders, and peers that you do not deserve — especially you do not deserve to have fun. These sources of learning were not necessarily ill-intentioned. Much of what they taught you was what they learned and what they thought would "protect" you from a world they didn't understand and therefore a world that seemed the be "the enemy." They did not want you to get your hopes up and have them dashed. They did not want you to get hurt, so they taught you that you did not deserve. Sometimes, they were ill-intentioned. Out of jealousy, possessiveness, and fear, some did intend to imprison you in their limitations. Whichever, you were taught, and you can "un-teach" yourself now.

"You can learn and work through the psychological and metaphysical obstacles that separate you from the reality you ask for.

"However, if you don't think you deserve, all of the above are intellectual exercises fast becoming exercises in frustration and futility."

2. You are haunted by angers, hurts, and resentments of the past. Separate from what you were innocently or maliciously taught, many are followed by the specter of the past. As a child you were so angry you wished your mother was dead. You numbed the hurt with hate. You harnessed the anguish with resentment. Lonely, you punished yourself. You decided you did not deserve to be happy. Ever! You still live by that decision. You are haunted by the past.

3. You feel guilty. The guilt you may feel can be sourced in fact and fantasy, or it can be unsourced in the belief that you are guilty just by being alive. Perhaps you were taught; perhaps you were conditioned. Now you feel guilty. According to you, you do not deserve. The possibility of happiness, the possibility of having fun, is frightening. It is a threat. This is where your lack of deserving lies if you find yourself feeling guilty when things go wrong and even worse — guiltier — when things go right. Are you constantly apologizing for being here — for being alive?

4. You are caught in the "catch-22" of deserving. You come to realize that the lack of deserving is the problem. You are eloquent and articulate about all the reasons you don't deserve. You have even worked at re-learning what the inner-child erroneously learned. You have released the haunting angers, hurts, resentments, and you have freed yourself from guilt. Yet you still don't feel you deserve. Why?

Because, you tell yourself, if you deserved, you would have figured it out long ago! You say you don't deserve because you still feel undeserving. You continue by telling yourself that if you were a person who was meant to feel deserving, you would have done it already. Wrapped in a negative ego of, "I'd hate to admit it," you are caught in a "catch-22" reality.

Often, there is a feeling of foolishness: "I should already know this. I should already have done this." Believe us, you will only feel more foolish to wait even another month. If you feel foolish now, how much more foolish are you going to feel in a year from now?

Admit your foolishness and your embarrassment. Break the "catch-22" by realizing you are not alone. Everyone feels the lack of deserving. It is part of your human condition. It is part of what you are learning through the lens, through the focus, of learning to have fun.

5. You are depressed. Depression is anger that you fear you will get in trouble for having. Many who are depressed in their marriages or relationships are often angry, but fear reprisals should they talk about it. Many who dread going to work because their jobs depress them are really saying they are angry, but actualization carries intolerable consequences. The anger that seeds depression can build over many months or many years, or it can come from quick and sudden change. One of the ways you suppress — repress — depress — that anger is by denying fun. You deny it by refusing it, or by choosing to believe that it is outside the realms of possibility or probability. Either way, it is beyond your reach.

6. You lack perfection. You have made mistakes, and you have not forgiven yourself. Perhaps you are waiting for others to forgive you or to apologize to you. Perhaps you have decided that you are unforgivable. Whatever you tell yourself, you have concluded that you do not deserve to have fun. Erroneously you have decided that you can have fun once you are perfect, and not before. Since you already have made a mistake, you are doomed. If you can discover the arrogance rather than feel the self-pity of this position, you can be free of it.

"Having fun involves learning to create your reality, defining the means and the ends you wish to achieve and acquire, balancing the future and the present against the backdrop of the past, and most of all involves allowing yourself to feel and then be deserving."

7. You decided you do not love "good enough." Like the lack of deserving you were taught, many of you have concluded that you simply do not love "good enough." In many situations, the Human Potential Movement and the ensuing metaphysics have fostered that conditioning. Many have decided that humankind as well as they, individually, have a fatal flaw — an original sin of sorts — of an inability to love. Because they can't love, or can't love "good enough," they do not deserve anything — especially they do not deserve to have fun. Nor, according to them, does anyone else.

We realize we have not offered concrete solutions and resolutions to these obstacles to your deserving. Knowing what stops you — knowing the hurdles and where they are — can be the first step in finding your own solutions.

Having fun is not the glib and shallow concept so many want to think it is. It sounds simple enough, yet your reality belies that suspected simplicity. After so many lifetimes, fun and learning how to have it seem as elusive as ever.

Having fun involves learning to create your reality, defining the means and the ends you wish to achieve and acquire, balancing the future and the present against the backdrop of the past, and most of all involves allowing yourself to feel and then be deserving.

With new and greater understanding: Learn to have fun!

*Paul Zuromski, **Body, Mind & Spirit**, Johnston, Rhode Island*

Success and Its Secrets

Lazaris: We have previously discussed the main reason for creating yourself and your physical world: To learn to have fun. The other essential purpose, mission, or task — or, as we call it, focus — is as important and as illusive as the first. The second focus: To learn to consciously create success.

You see, it is not just about being successful. It is about learning. It is about being conscious. It is about defining exactly what success is for you.

Creating your own reality is something you do whether you are conscious of it or not. Everyone consciously creates their own reality. Some, lost in the labyrinth of ignorance or naiveté, do not know it. Others, caught in the web of fear and ridicule, deny it. Many, trapped in the paralysis of being *in potentia*, wish it were true. Regardless, you do create your own reality.

Conscious creation of reality is how you function. Conscious creation of success is where you focus.

We do not want to examine the entire arena of creating success. That has been done. The bookshelves of your reality are replete with the "how-to's" of success.

We want to plant seeds of consideration to help you more clearly understand what success really is for you, and how to more concretely be able to consciously create it for yourself.

To begin, we must look at what success isn't. Many of you don't really know what success is. It is one of those concepts that you are supposed to "just know." Potential humiliation overrules curiosity. Without clear understanding you continuously seek and never find success.

Q: So much of the New Age tries to focus on success. I'd like your comments. You say it's the second focus. Please explain. Please talk about success.

In lieu of clarity you accept the consensus reality definitions thinking that success means greater intelligence, more deserving, and "better than." You assume success entails competing with others and conquering scarcity. Success is concomitant with perfection in action and intention.

*"The most elegant definition of power is **the ability and the willingness to act."***

Initially this sounds acceptable — even preferable. In time, you realize that you are not meeting these standards. No matter how intelligent you are, there are those who are smarter. You don't feel deserving. No matter how persuasive you are, no matter how many others you convince, you cannot convince yourself that you deserve — that you really deserve. No matter how tightly you hold on to your "better thans," they keep slipping through your fingers. Competing and conquering are not only exhaustive, they're boring. You are not perfect. You are not perfect. No, you're not.

To stop the erosion, you simplify your consensus reality definitions. Success means having more and better than, being more and better than, doing more and better than. Success means more ... !

Shuddering at the prospect of failure, you take a deep breath, you steel yourself, and you dive in again. Rather than realizing that the definitions are incorrect, you try again to make them work for you. Some will spend their whole lives on this merry-go-round reaching for a brass ring that isn't there. Never was, never will be.

"Um-pa-pa, Um-pa-pa." There is no end. What success you do create feels like a fluke that can be snatched away at any moment. As much as failure is painful, success is more frightening. There is no real success on the merry-go-round.

Some reluctantly get off the carousel by being knocked off with the hard edge of failure. They judge, punish, and conclude that they are no good. They feel and are convinced that they "blew it — it's too late."

Then there are those who are forced off the carousel by getting caught in the soft vice of self-delusion or by getting lost in the mirrored maze of grandeur. They convince themselves that they have met the criteria. The euphoria is eventually replaced with the haunting hollowness: "Is this all there is?"

A few, a very few, consciously climb off the merry-go-round by releasing the consensus reality definitions. Admitting that they do not know what success is, they then search for new meaning and create their own definitions of success — of their success.

The most effective way to define success in a way that the definition can be your definition, is to lay forth the core — the backbone — the backbone of what success is. The skeleton of success is just that: a skeleton. You must give it life by adding the flesh and blood, the muscle and nerve, and the thinking and feeling of success. You must breath life into these pieces of the puzzle called success.

"Creativity is generating and stimulating conception and perception in yourself and/or in others."

Not surprisingly, there are seven basic components to being successful. You all know these seven pieces of the puzzle. Often, you just don't know how they fit together.

1. First is power. The most elegant definition of power is *the ability and the willingness to act.* Power, in truth, has nothing to do with intimidation, control, or manipulation. It has nothing to do with the desire or the attempts to overpower.

"Power" has become a euphemism for fear. When you confront a scary person you often call them powerful. When you encounter a powerful person you often call them scary! Very strange.

True power is being both able and willing to choose and decide, and to act on those choices and decisions. It is being able and willing to think and feel and act on those thoughts and emotions. It is being able and willing to admit to having attitudes (opinions, evaluations, and discernments) and beliefs and then acting consciously on those attitudes and beliefs.

2. The second puzzle piece is creativity and productivity. Creativity is generating and stimulating conception and perception in yourself and/or in others. Creativity is not defined by career or label. The artist and the non-artist, by whatever definition, are creative if they generate and stimulate conception and perception.

Levels of productivity are measured by the amount you learn about yourself. Whatever you are doing, if you learn a great deal about you and who you are, then it is productive. If you learn little or nothing, then it is nonproductive. Productivity is a quality, not a quantity.

3. Then there is awareness, and there is aliveness. Many look for lofty esoteric meanings for these two concepts. In their search they lose sight of success. To be aware, concisely, means knowing you have impact. Some believe that it is impossible to have impact on each other. Some limit it to not being able to have negative impact on each other. Yet others will concede and deal with the impact. Whether they are supposed to have it or not, they actually do have impact on the people around them. Regardless, everyone agrees that you have impact, at least on yourself. When you know this — really know this — you become aware.

When you combine four very special ingredients, something very special happens. You create the synergy of aliveness. Synergy means the whole is greater than the sum of the parts, and in this case the aliveness is more than just equal parts of *love, trust, expectancy,* and *enthusiasm.*

To become really alive it is important to combine the flexibility and fluidity of love with the fragility and rigidity of trust. Then it is vital to stir in the wonder of expectancy and the sparkle of enthusiasm. Mix well. Be alive.

4. Happiness is the fulfillment of your needs. Joy is the fulfillment of your preferences. Enjoyment is the elegance with which you do both.

5. Many make the mistake of assuming that success means having resources. In truth, success means having *access* to resources. There are those who have money, but no real access to it or to what it can buy them. They do not experience success. Others have loads of access to money as their only resource. They often experience limited or shallow success. The truly successful person will have expansive access to physical and metaphysical resources. Success is within the grasp of anyone who can close their eyes, alter their state of consciousness, visualize, and manifest in their reality. If you are willing, each of you has unlimited potential access to all the resources — unlimited potentials for success.

6. Critical to being successful: the willingness to adventure.

In your "old age" world you learn to be a warrior. You learn to confront, to battle, to conquer, and you dominate. In the "New Age" world you can learn to be an adventurer. You can learn to encounter, to understand, to befriend, and to transmute with dominion. Consciously created success involves — integrally involves — being willing to adventure in your reality and in your world.

7. Dominion is an attitude and a belief. Dominion is a point of view. When you are willing to co-create your success with God/Goddess/All That Is rather than expecting someone to do it for you, you are on your way.

"In your 'old age' world you learn to be a warrior. ... In the 'New Age' world you can learn to be an adventurer. You can learn to encounter, to understand, to befriend, and to transmute with dominion."

When you are willing to stretch and reach for the future rather than grovel in the past, you begin to feel the excitement and the wonder of dominion. When you are able to see and demonstrate that first your world — and then the world-at-large — is a friendly place ready to support you rather than out to get you, then you have dominion.

With dominion, you have the final piece of the puzzle called success.

The secret of being successful — of learning to be successful? Begin by owning each of the seven puzzle pieces as an attitude first. *Feel.* Feel powerful, creative/productive, aware/alive. Feel happiness and joy in an enjoying way. Feel that you have access to resources, a willingness to adventure. Feel dominion.

Do not expect to be successful first and then to have the feeling. Feel it first. Feel it first.

Do not aim at being successful. Do not make success the bull's eye of your target. Don't "shoot for success." Ironically, the secret to consciously creating success is not to make it the central target of your desire, expectation, or imagination. Rather, accomplish the means. Aim to be powerful, creative/productive, etc. Aim at the means and allow the ends to follow.

Don't shoot for the ends. Accomplish the means. The ends will follow.

Paul Zuromski, **Body, Mind & Spirit,** *Johnston, Rhode Island*

The Success Cube

Lazaris: The secret to consciously creating success is not to make it the central target of your desire, expectation, or imagination. As we suggested previously, aim at being powerful, creative/productive, and aware/alive. Seek the enjoyment/happiness/joy, the access to resources, and be willing to adventure. Open your mind and heart to dominion.

As you aim at the means of success, the ends — the actual manifestation — can occur. The ends will follow.

What if they don't? The techniques work. Too many people have created too much success with our suggestions. You can't fault the technique. The concepts are sound. Metaphysics works. What if success doesn't happen? There are basically four things you can do.

You can blame yourself which leads to blaming others — someone or something. To do this you must retreat into a consensus reality definition of success. You must rely on a "less-than/more-than" continuum in order to assess blame — even to blame yourself. This approach may appeal to many, but we do not recommend it because it only defers responsibility, which eventually you will take. And it is a lie.

You can rummage around your fears of failure. However, we caution you: Failure is not as scary as it used to be. After all, you have, each of you, dealt with failure many times. In many ways, though unpleasant, it is familiar. It is fashionable to fear failure. It can be valuable if you discover a thread or root of humiliation, perfection, or peer pressure that trips you up. We would look, but not dwell. Do not get caught up in your fears of failure.

Q: Even when we understand the importance as well as the benefit of being successful, it's just not that easy. What stops us, Lazaris, and what can we do about it?

It is much more valuable to evaluate your fears of success. In your explorations of human potential, you have encountered or confronted the idea of fearing success.

There are numerous fears associated with succeeding. Some of the most common:

1) Fear of Responsibility for creating, maintaining, and sustaining the success once created. It's easier to be mediocre, for there is always potential improvement and praise. When you get the "A", however, you must maintain and sustain. The initial praise quickly turns to whispers and then is hushed.

2) Fear of Freedom from the past. You often have spoken or unspoken "failure-loyalty pacts" with family, friends, or with a destructive image of yourself. Honored, they imprison.

3) Fear of Boredom, the fear that life will lose its zest and appeal. Is there life after ambition? After success, what's left? Not knowing can scare you.

4) Fear of Usury/Betrayal accompanies success. When you look at a successful person and think that it is all right to use them because "they can afford it" or "they should expect it by now," you are setting your own fears in motion. When you think you will be nicer, more attentive, or laugh a little more with a successful person because they are successful, when you want to be around a successful person in hopes that it will "rub off" or that you will benefit by "being in their wake," you are creating your own fears of being used or betrayed when you become successful.

5) Fear of Loneliness is like a fog. So much of your interaction with friends is about overcoming failure or about creating success. Once done, what do you talk about? What is the foundation of your friendships? Is there room to be successful? How often have you heard:

"Yes, but are they happy? They may be rich, but look how lonely ..."

6) Fear of Visibility frightens many. There is a fear of criticism and ridicule. There is a fear of humiliation and rejection, not for failing — as we say you have done that many times — but for succeeding.

7) Fear of the Future creates its own limiter of success. We have often said: The problem is *not* that the world is going to be destroyed and that there will be no future; rather, the problem is that the world *won't* be destroyed and there *will* be a world and a future for which *you* are going to be responsible.

"Many of you can create success, but you reach a limit and the success either stops or it falls away. It is almost as if you bump into a ceiling or something."

The fourth thing you can do is to look at your Success Cube. The Success Cube is a concept that we introduced to more fully explain the phenomenon of success.

Many of you can create success, but you reach a limit and the success either stops or it falls away. It is almost as if you bump into a ceiling or something.

Others of you can create seemingly unlimited success in certain arenas of your life, and have absolutely no success in other areas. It's like the success is contained or bottled up. It does not spill over into the rest of your life.

Most of you are running as fast as you can and, successful or not, it is just not working. It is just not working any more!

Inadequate explanations give way to hackneyed phrases which, in turn, give way to "ho-hum" shrugs and absent shakes of the head. The search for meaning deteriorates to a breathy resolve to try again. "Maybe it will be different this time," is punctuated with a heave and a sigh rather than an exclamation!

Each of you has a limit to your success. Those limits can be defined by blame or by fears of failure and success. However, one of the most controlling and unknown limiters of success is defined by the dimensions of success: your Success Cube.

In a three-dimensional reality it only makes sense that your success would have three dimensions. It makes sense, but you seldom consider more than one dimension: how much. If that fails, then: how many.

"Depth is the emotional and aesthetic richness YOU receive from your success. It is the creativity and productivity you stimulate in yourself. It is the hope and courage that the success, with all its height and width, gives you. It is the peace."

Your success has height which is the measure of how much. How much prestige, money, position, possession, or ... The criteria are set by your outward image, your assessment of how others see you and how you want to be seen by others. The height of your success is also determined by your beliefs and your attitudes about yourself, about success, and about the relationship between the two.

Most of you understand height. Your fear of success is often a fear of heights.

The width of your success is a measure of how many — a measure of the number of areas in which you allow yourself the experience and the benefit of success. Some will be successful at work, with a very unsuccessful home or personal live. Or vice versa. Some will be intellectually superb and an emotional clutz! Not vice versa, though.

The width of your success is based upon your deservability — how much you honestly think and feel that you deserve to be successful. It is also the manifestation of your thoughts and feelings about the concepts and the facts of success.

A lot of old wives with their tales have limited the width of your success. Your fear of success is often a fear of stepping outside your boundaries.

The depth of success is the dimension that most of you ignore. You can understand the height and width of success, but the depth eludes you. Yes it does. It eludes you in life as well.

Depth is the emotional and aesthetic richness YOU receive from your success. It is the creativity and productivity you stimulate in yourself. It is the hope and courage that the success, with all its height and width, gives you. It is the peace.

You give love, and you work on receiving love. How often do you stop and just let yourself be loved? How often do you allow yourself to change because you know somebody loves you? That is the richness — the depth — of success.

This elusive dimension comes from the choices and decisions you make about yourself and your interaction — your interface — with success. The choices and decisions you make about your encounter with success define the depth. Your depth is also determined by your internal image — not how you want others to see you or how others actually do see you, but how you honestly see yourself.

The lack of depth is why your success is never enough even though everyone tells you that you should be happy. The frustration of unfulfillment is a lack of depth. The circles that never become spirals — when you feel like you are going around and around and staying in the same place, never improving, never learning more, or never expanding — the circles that never become spirals define the shallowness.

The shallowness haunts. The lack of depth haunts, erodes, and eventually conquers success. All success.

You ask what to do about it?

1. Define your Cube of Success. Define it as an abstract, as it applies to life — your life. Also, honestly look at your Success Cubes (plural) in the various areas, arenas, of your life. What is your Success Cube around work, around love, around friendship, around

recreation, around your spirituality? Each Cube may be different. You need to know.

Use meditation to define and describe the three dimensions — height, width, and depth — of your success. Also use pencil and paper. You may need to practice drawing. More importantly, you may need to practice honesty.

In your heart and mind, and then on paper, draw your Cube and Cubes. Look, understand, and perceive.

2. Recognize that you created this Cube out of the raw materials of reality — beliefs/attitudes (the height), thoughts/feelings (the width), and decisions/choices (the depth). You did it. It was also your outward and inward image and your issues of deserving that determined the Cube and Cubes, but you dictated the terms. You did it!

Acknowledge that it was you. Others may have given you the raw materials and the substance of those materials, but you took them and you continued to use them. They are yours. Acknowledge it for yourself.

Then forgive yourself for the Cube and Cubes you have created. Forgive yourself for living there. Forgive yourself for the prison you made and for imprisoning yourself.

Give yourself permission to change.

3. Meditatively get inside your existing Cube. If it is high with very little width and virtually no depth, then be inside this shaft-like cylinder. If you have lots of width with no height or depth, then feel yourself lying down in your coffin-like Cube. If your height is okay and the width is acceptable, notice how flat you feel — how "up against it" you feel.

Be inside your Cube. As uncomfortable as it is: LIVE WITH IT! You have been living with it so far; a little more is only going to help.

4. Stretch your Cube. In the meditation, do what you have to do to change the shape and size. SHAPE AND SIZE. Redesign your Cube. Give it what it lacks. Work with all the dimensions.

If you only make it higher, you may lose volume in the width or depth. You may create more money or recognition, but pay for it in your home, friendships, recreation, or spiritual success. You may pay for the added height by eliminating any emotional or aesthetic richness that was there already.

To increase only the width can cost you in height and depth. To add only depth is martyrhood!

Increase ALL dimensions with attention to those which are lacking. Create a new Cube and a new series of Cubes.

The subconscious understands the pictures you create far more than the words you might say. The subconscious will understand and respond.

A final thought: As well as stretching your Cube in meditation, stretch it in fact. What are the beliefs/attitudes and images that define the height of your success? Change the pictures, and change the stuff of which the pictures are made.

Work with your thoughts/feelings and decisions/choices so that you can fill the new Success Cube you have created.

Find the walls. You may not see them with your eyes, but you can see and feel them with your heart and with your mind. You can move them with your desire, expectation, and imagination ... and your imagination ... and your imagination.

Paul Zuromski, **Body, Mind & Spirit,** *Johnston, Rhode Island*

Our Aspiration

Q: Should we
aspire to be
like Lazaris?
Should we
aspire to be
without a
body?

Lazaris: Eventually you will expand your consciousness beyond the limitations of form. Growth is not linear. So, when you are "done with the body," it's not as though you're going to leave it behind as you might leave a friendship behind, or leave a town behind when you move on, or a job behind when you quit and move to a better position. No. In growth it's like a pebble being dropped into a pond: The ripple goes in all directions. So when you grow, you grow beyond physicalness, not linearly but exponentially, such that you grow around it.

To use another analogy, it is like the seed of a pearl. The seed is a grain of sand. Within the beauty of that pearl, in the lustre of that pearl, at the very core of it is that grain of sand. That grit began it all. Growth expands in all directions. So you never lose your physicalness. You simply expand your awareness beyond it so much so that other things become so much more primary that you "forget it."

Should you aspire to be like us? No. No, no, no, no! No! Absolutely not! Aspire to be more like you. It is not to follow us or to become like us, or to hope someday that you are us ... no.

We would encourage you to become more like you, and to be like a friend. You look up to various friends. You admire this quality in them, that quality in them, and you say, "Gee, I'd like to have more of that in me." But it becomes more of "you" in you, in your expression of generosity, your expression of caring, your expression of love. "I see this person, and I would like to be more loving, but it'll be my characteristic of loving —

not to mimic or copy them — but to express what I am in that energy."

So to the extent that we might be friends, we suggest, there might be certain qualities in us that you would like to aspire to, or like to have as your own, but when you express those same energies, they will not be Lazaris' love, or Lazaris' giving, or Lazaris' caring. They'll be your love and your giving and your caring. Therefore, no, don't aspire to be us. Aspire to be more of who you are, in that regard, and that's what we would encourage.

*Craig Steel, **Together Books**, Denver*

Humanity: The Next Step

Lazaris: Overall humanity is doing wonderfully well. One has to look really at two levels: There is the consensus humanity, which, of course, would be — for lack of a better definition — all the peoples of the world, which exponentially comprise humanity.

Please allow a slight digression: Society is the arithmetic combination of people — numbers, megasociety, in that particular regard — whereas humanity is not arithmetic, but rather exponential. There's an energy that is more than just people. There is something that is due to the togetherness of those people — due not just to the quantity of them, but to the quality of them. Therefore, the consensus humanity, that exponential energy that is all people, is moving along in its very lumbering and encumbering way, which is to be expected.

Within that consensus humanity there is a sliver of reality, there is a little light beam, a laser-like beam of light that comprises those who are enlightened or be-

Q: From your perspective, how is humanity doing in this period of growth and enlightenment, of raising our consciousness, of heading home?

coming enlightened (more clearly put). That light is made up of those that are interested in the New Age, those that are interested in expanding consciousness, those that are interested in finding solutions to "solutionless" problems.

The light is made up of those who are looking to figure out the Rubik's Cube of reality that you're currently in — not giving up on it and throwing up their hands and saying, "There must be no solution." Rather, they know that: "There are solutions. We just haven't been willing to dream them yet. We just haven't found the proper perspective. We haven't found the proper questions to ask. But there are solutions."

That sliver of people, that sliver of humanity that is involved in the New Age, is doing incredibly well. They're moving forward quite nicely despite all the encumbrances, despite the fears, despite the doubts and angers that have been thrown in the path, unfortunately, by some of those people who claim to lead them.

"... your Earth has an incredible capacity to love, even despite your fighting and your warring and your perpetual violence. Underneath it there is a tremendous passion and compassion to love."

Overall people are becoming much more discerning and much more willing to grow, much more legitimate in their growth. That wedge is growing. That sliver of light is becoming wider and wider as more and more people from all walks of life are opening themselves up not to the crazy sort of fanciful parts of this metaphysical community, but to the sincerity and earnestness of what metaphysics, of what spirituality, of what a relationship with God — as we call it God/Goddess/All That Is — can actually lead to. Therefore, both that particular ray of energy within humanity and all of humanity-at-large are moving forward.

We have often said that human beings are so incredibly beautiful. You have been taught that you are somewhat the barnacles, somewhat at the bottom of the pile, that somehow all these extraterrestrials that people claim are there are coming around to help you because you are so unable to do it for yourselves. You have been taught that you're falling so far behind that if you don't catch up you're going to have a devastating impact upon the whole cosmos. All these kinds of guilt-producing messages are given forth.

We suggest, quite to the contrary, that many of those so-called extraterrestrials that are here observing you are *not* observing you to teach you. They're observing to learn from you, because there's something rather incredible about you and your planet Earth. You and it are filled with a tremendous urge to be spiritual. You are filled with a tremendous seeking of God/Goddess/All That Is or whatever name you call the Source. A tremendous seeking in that way is common to and is unique to your planet.

"... for the whole world is watching to see what you do. The whole world is waiting for you to love."

Also, your Earth has an incredible capacity to love, even despite your fighting and your warring and your perpetual violence. Underneath it there is a tremendous passion and compassion to love. Within the United States there is an incredible capacity. The American people are perhaps the fastest to forgive of any peoples in the world. Injustices and wrongdoings have been done, but your nation, above all, forgives and goes back to loving quicker than any place else. In your nation, more than in any other part of the world, we would dare say, there is such a tremendous urge to grow, a tremendous urge to find the answers, a tremendous urge to seek and find that God, or that God/Goddess/All That Is, or that Source of life and reality.

Many have thought of Tibet and the Himalayan Mountains as the source or the seed of spirituality, and indeed it was. But we suggest that has shifted. It's in the Western World, and in the Western World most specifically the United States, where that seed of power, that source of spiritual urging, is located.

Yes, humanity is moving forward incredibly well and will succeed in creating the successful reality that many of the doomsdayers have dismissed as being impossible.

*Paul Zuromski, **Body, Mind & Spirit**, Johnston, Rhode Island*

Q: For those of us involved in the New Age or, as you call it, The New Spirituality, what should we be doing now?

Lazaris: It is going to be very important for those of you involved, truly, in the spiritual search, who are involved in this metaphysical/spiritual world, to stretch and to reach and to look for the positive, and to look for the opportunities of success. For you will become the pioneers. You will become, as we call them, the Mapmakers. You will be the ones that the rest of the world will lean upon, will look to for guidance and for understanding. When your world of objectivity becomes subjective, when your world of subjectivity becomes objective, when indeed what seems to be up becomes down, and back and forth (not in a polar shift, as some have suggested, but in a change of consciousness), there will be many who will turn to you. Don't look back and say, "I told you so." Reach out with love, reach out with understanding, reach out with the compassion and the passion that you have for life and for the wonders that that life can hold.

This is the grandest time of all to be alive, for this is the beginning of that New Age in a bigger, more profound way than it has ever begun for any individual in the past. Therefore, you are witness to a time in history that has never been and a time in history that will never be again.

You are not only witness to it, but also you are a part of it. As we like to say, reach and stretch and allow yourself to be the brightest light that you can be, for the whole world is watching to see what you do. The whole world is waiting for you to love.

*Paul Zuromski, **Body, Mind & Spirit**, Johnston, Rhode Island*

With love and peace ...

Lazaris

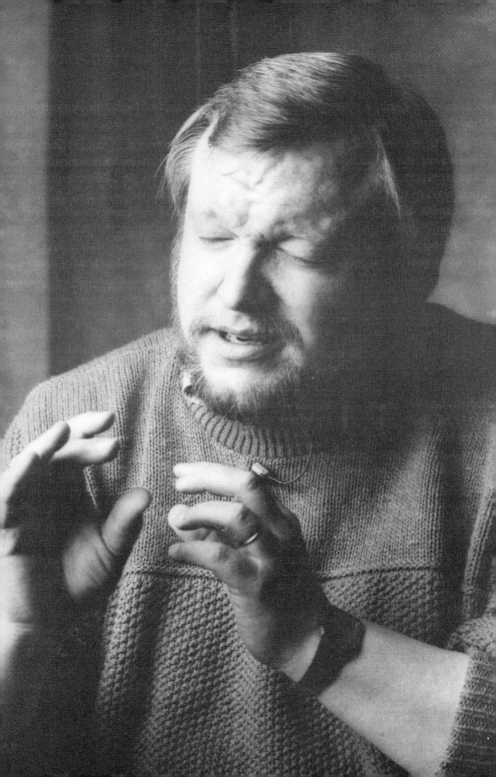

Death & Reincarnation

Other Lives, Other Times — Karma — Death

Other Lives, Other Times

Q: Lazaris, would you talk to us about reincarnation and past and parallel lifetimes?

Lazaris: You know, as metaphysicians, that your Physical Plane is an illusion. You know as astute, intelligent people — whether you're metaphysical or not — that reality is an illusion. Your scientists have demonstrated this so conclusively, so repetitively, so rigidly, that the only way you can pretend otherwise is to deny the truth. The metaphysicians and the scientists, who are usually at odds with one another, agree totally on this issue: Your reality is a product of thought. Your reality is a product of consciousness. Your reality is an illusion of light. Your reality is an illusion.

Metaphysicians from the beginning of time have said: Time is an illusion. Einstein demonstrated that time is an illusion. Subsequent quantum physicists have more than demonstrated and proved that time is an illusion, that it is a convenience you have created for yourself. All things are simultaneous. Every lifetime you have is occuring now. Every lifetime you have is occuring now.

Now you have those lifetimes, and you put them on a continuum. You call the left end of this continuum the past, and you call the right end of it the future. All that really means is that you are putting the whole array of lifetimes that are randomly scattered or placed out there — the entire *smörgåsbord* of lifetimes — in order. You are putting them in sequence.

Following the analogy of a *smörgåsbord*, when you go to a cafeteria, do you ever notice that while standing at the beginning of the line all the food is there? Even though you can't get to it all at once — even though you put it on your plate in sequence — it is still all there. And you go down the line, don't you? And of course, what do they put first? The desserts! ... {laughter} ... They put the desserts first. Then they put salads, boring salads. White lettuce. It's an amazing thing, white lettuce. ... {laughter} ... Then they put all the steamed main courses. Then they put the bread and butter and drinks and things like this. And you go down the line, and you gather a plateful of food. Do you eat the dessert first? Maybe some of you ... {laughter} ... You tend to do it like you're supposed to. You start with the salad. Then you eat the main course. Then you eat your dessert. But it's all there on your tray, and it's all there on the *smörgåsbord* or in the cafeteria line. Whether you are at the beginning, middle, or the end of the line, it's all there at once.

Well, your lifetimes are like that, too, all laid out. They're all there. You choose. "I'm going to do this one, and then I'm going to follow it with this one, and then I'm going to follow it with that one." You give yourself time. Sometimes your next lifetime might be in Atlantis, or it might be in the Middle Ages, or it might be in the 1800s. They're all there. They're all there, and you pick and choose which ones you want to experience when you want to experience them.

The other analogy we use is a movie theatre. Particularly your multiple cinemas are conducive to this. When you go to a multiple cinema, sometimes all the movies are playing at the same time. You can go to this one and that one and this one and that one — any order you want. They're all playing.

So lifetimes are that way. You have those that are called past and present and future lifetimes that are those which are in the same space as you, but in different times, and that's your illusion. You also have those lifetimes that are called parallel lifetimes, which are in the same time, but in a different space. There's a "you"

"All lifetimes are simultaneous — past, present, future, parallel, overlapping. All of them are happening at once."

that's alive now that isn't this you, but is a parallel to you. It's not literally a geometric parallel, but it's a "parallel" to you in time, not space. Some of you have two or three parallel lifetimes. A "you" might be living in New York City right now, a best-selling author living on Fifth Avenue with a view of the park or whatever. A parallel life is a split-off of you.

Often split-offs occur in your adolescence because those are the times that you are highly filled with fantasy. Some of you, when you were 13, could have "died" to be a doctor, right? You watched every doctor show. You read every doctor book. A doctor — that's what you were going to be — a doctor, a doctor, a doctor, a doctor, a doctor! Then one day something happened, and ... "Doctor? I don't want to be a doctor!" It's as though it disappeared.

Often what has happened is you've split off, and that part of you, who has the same parents and the same upbringing, splits off and lives a totally different life, let's say as a doctor at Columbia University in New York City, or wherever. But if you went to New York, if you looked them up in the roster, you'd never find them, because although they're in the same time, they're in a different space. Those are parallel lifetimes.

You have past lifetimes and parallel lifetimes. Your parallel lifetimes have past lifetimes and your past lifetimes also have their parallel lifetimes.

Assume that you have a past lifetime where you live and die as a corner grocer in Chicago, 1880 - 1960. You have your current lifetime doing whatever you do, and you were born in Pittsburgh in 1940. For those 20 years, — from 1940 to 1960 — the two lifetimes overlap. There are overlapping lifetimes that you have because all the lifetimes are happening at once. Time is an illusion. All lifetimes are simultaneous — past, present, future, parallel, overlapping. All of them are happening at once.

The most correct way would be to refer to all lifetimes as concurrent lives experienced in varying time/space continua. That is rather bulky, so you call them past, present, future, parallel, or overlapping. This is technically incorrect, but it is efficient and effective. Like time itself, it is an illusion that is technically incorrect, but both efficient and effective.

"Well, why bother about past lifetimes?" Exactly. Why bother? ... {laughter} ... Some of you have no interest in them. Fine, don't bother! The Channel has no particular interest in his past lifetimes. We did a life reading for him one time. We made a cassette tape for him at Peny's request. He listened to it once and said, "Hmm." And that was it. ... {laughter} ...

What about those of you who have had life readings? Should you not have done so? No. If you're interested in lives, then learn about them. What we suggest, and we make this very clear whenever we talk of past lives, is that lifetimes do not *cause*. They do not cause your current life. They influence. They *influence*.

We've used the analogy of a sunburn, where if you're sunburned and someone slaps you sharply on the back ... "Oh!" It's going to sting. It's going to make you cry. It's going to make you hate for a moment or two until you can control yourself. ... {laughter} ...

If you have no sunburn on the back and someone slaps you sharply, it's going to sting, but not as much. It may annoy you. "Why do they have to be like that!" It may cause some irritation, but not hate.

What caused the pain? Sunburn? No. No. The sunburn did not cause the pain. The slap on the back caused the pain. The sunburn influenced the intensity.

"Lifetimes ... can influence each other, but they do not control. They do not cause. Therefore, if you failed in a past lifetime, it does not mean you will fail now. But if you do fail now ... the fact that you failed previously may influence what you do — how you handle it now."

Lifetimes are like sunburn. They can influence each other, but they do not control. They do not cause. Therefore, if you failed in a past lifetime, it does not mean you will fail now. But if you do fail now, if you do create failure now ("now" is the only place you can create anything anyway), the fact that you failed previously may influence what you do — how you handle it now. For some of you it may influence in such a way that you can handle the failure more smoothly. "No problem. I don't know why, but I know exactly what to do about it." Because of the influence of the past, you are prepared to handle this one easily. Others may feel totally devastated because the previous failure produces an influence of feeling more fearful.

Lifetimes can influence, just as you and a friend can influence each other. But you cannot honestly control each other. What you do does not make them, does not control them. It can influence them. Lifetimes are like friends.

Anonymous Question, Evening with Lazaris, Atlanta, 1987

Q: Do you and your probable selves actualize the same events?

Lazaris: You do not ever meet a parallel lifetime, and you tend not to run into your overlapping lifetimes, because the trauma would be just too disconcerting. No, you don't run into them, and they don't have the same events.

Overlapping lifetimes are lifetimes where the previous one has not quite ended when the next one begins. The end of one overlaps the beginning of another. Sometimes your favorite television shows overlap, or two movies that you want to see on the same night overlap. It is disconcerting, isn't it?

Well, you do sometimes experience the same phenomenon in lifetimes since they are all simultaneous. One begins before the other ends, except with lifetimes you generally aren't aware of the overlap because it would be too confusing. It would be too confusing for a 5-year-old child to encounter or confront the 80-year-old man they are/were/are in a previous lifetime. It would be really disconcerting. They'd lock you up — either as the old man realizing "I'm a 5-year-old child," or as a 5-year-old child realizing, "I'm an old man!" Either way, you're in trouble!

So therefore, you bury even the intuition or remembrance of such things. Shhhh! Don't even talk about that stuff, you know? Anyway, even if you did have an intuitive "hit," by the time you're six or seven you forget about it anyway, so we would suggest you aren't aware of probable selves like that. No, you don't run into them, and they don't have the same events.

Anonymous Question, Evening with Lazaris, Seattle, 1987

Karma

L azaris: Yes. Well, what about *karma?* Time is an illusion. Do we all agree on that? Is there anyone who doesn't agree? Anyone think time is real? Because, you see, Einstein proved that it was an illusion. Scientists subsequently have proved it's an illusion.

Q: Lazaris, would you talk to us about karma?

You have only straightened out time in the last 500 years to accommodate your Renaissance and to satisfy scientific and Judeo-Christian ethics. Both rely very heavily on a beginning and an end of reality — on a beginning and an end of time. Both need time to be a straight line.

Prior to 500 years ago time was a spiral, and it was created to serve you and assist you. It can still be of service as a convenience. "Let's get together at 8:00 tonight" makes sense.

"Let's get together at frum-frum." ... {laughter} ...

"What time?"

"Um-hmmm-hmmm." ... {laughter} ...

"Well, we'll just flow with it, all right?"

So you create time to say, "Let's do it Sunday the 13th at 8:00 p.m." It's much more convenient that way. So you create time as the illusion of convenience. Time is an illusion, which means there is no "then," and there is no "before," and there is no "after." There is only now.

So tell us about *karma?* What is *karma? Karma* is called the Law of Cause and Effect. *Karma* is supposedly the law that says what you did *then* you are paying for *now*. Now wait a minute. We all agreed there is no such thing as time, and therefore what happened then and what happens now are all happening at the same time.

You say, "If you murdered someone in another lifetime, then you're going to have to get murdered in this one." Poppycock! Absolute sheer nonsense! If you get murdered in this lifetime, and you murdered someone in that lifetime, both events are happening simultaneously. How could one cause the other? How could that happen? It can't. It can't! Therefore, this idea that what you did in your past lifetimes you're paying for now is a philosophical—political—metaphysical statement, not an accurate one.

"What happened to the Jewish people in World War II should not be devalued or trivialized like that, should not be thrown away as some sort of karmic thing to be dismissed. It is far more important than that."

Where does the Law of Karma come from? Primarily it comes for most of you out of Eastern religion. Now here again, think about it. Imagine: Here you are the Holy Man, right, and here are your 4,000,000 followers who are starving, who have miserable lives, who exist in absolute abject poverty. So what do you tell them? "Well, you created this because you don't love yourself good enough." Oh! Talk about a self-destructive statement! You'll get stampeded, yes? Absolutely. ... {laughter} ... So instead you say, "Ummm, all your suffering now? Be glad for it because you're burning off *karma*. You must have been some rotten-to-the-core human being based on the *karma* that you're burning off, but nonetheless you're burning off *karma*, and every lifetime after lifetime after lifetime filled with misery is burning off *karma*."

What on Earth did you do that was so horrible that you deserve 40, 50, 60, 100 lifetimes of misery! Good grief! No, that's what you say to placate millions of people when you can hear the growl of their stomachs and see the starvation in their eyes. It's what you do when you know of no way to silence the growl or end the starvation.

"You're burning off karma. There was a time that you were gluttonous and ate too much, and now you're burning it off. There was a time when you deprived people of their food, and you're burning it off."

Some suggest that the Jews in World War II were the Romans that threw the Christians to the lions. No. What happened to the Jewish people in World War II should not be devalued or trivialized like that, should not be thrown away as some sort of *karmic* thing to be dismissed. It is far more important than that.

What happened to six million Jews and 12 million Russians and 11 million witches throughout your history should not be just thrown off as *"karma"*

"What happened to six million Jews and 12 million Russians and 11 million witches throughout your history should not be just thrown off as karma because it's not."

because it's not. All things are simultaneous. There is no such thing as the Law, the Law of Karma. There is a kind of *karmic* choice that you create for yourself. That's the importance: a *karmic* choice, not a law.

You see, you may have done something dastardly in a past lifetime, and you decide, "Look, I've got to work on that. I can't let that stand. I want to fix that." You may have betrayed someone, and therefore said, "I can't walk away from that. I am choosing, I am deciding, I am believing that I want to pay for that. I want to pay for that by going through it myself."

Now we ask you, if you cut off someone's finger and afterwards you feel *What did I do?*, does cutting off your own finger fix it? No, it doesn't. Does cutting off two fingers fix it? How about cutting off your hand at your wrist? Does that fix that? It doesn't fix it, does it? What does? Any ideas?

Forgive yourself. As you forgive yourself and apologize to them, on whatever level you need to do that, that's what fixes it. That's what fixes it. So you may have done betraying and dastardly things in your past, absolutely. And you may have failed miserably at love, and you may have failed miserably at power, and you may have been an oppressive person, and you decided, "In this lifetime I want to deal with love, and I want to learn about oppression, and I want to deal with this, and I want to deal with that, and I want to deal with power." But that's your choice — not the imposition of *karma*. That's your choice.

Therefore, *karma* does exist as long as you believe in it, and as soon as you're willing to drop it, it's gone. Not as soon as someone gives you permission, but rather as soon as you're willing to drop it, it's gone. So yes, you do have *karma*, because you chose it. God didn't impose it.

> "Karma does exist as long as you believe in it, and as soon as you're willing to drop it, it's gone. Not as soon as someone gives you permission, but rather as soon as you're willing to drop it, it's gone."

Some say *karma* is a law. We say it is a choice. We encourage you to think for yourself. You know time is a simultaneous illusion. Therefore, how can something happen before and something happen after? It is all happening now. How can something cause something else when both are simultaneous? How could there be *karmic* law? How could you be paying retribution for a lifetime that's happening right now? No, *karma* is not a law. It is a choice.

An example: Assume you were betrayed in a previous lifetime, and you also were betrayed in this lifetime. How you respond to that current betrayal may be influenced by that past betrayal. Some may handle it poorly because "it's happened to me before." Others may handle it superbly because "it's happened to me before." How will you handle it? It's not written in a book: "All betrayal will be handled this way." No, it's not. You decide how you're going to handle it.

If you were betrayed before and are betrayed now, the cause of that current betrayal is now, and you choose whether the previous betrayal is going to make it worse or if the previous betrayal is going to make it easier. It's your choice, not the law. And when you can realize this, then you can let go, and you're done with the "Wheel of the 84."

You're done with *karma* when you allow yourself to let it go, just like you're done with physical lifetimes when you can decide you're done, when you can realize, "I've learned enough. I didn't really *have* to learn anything at all. I chose to learn, and I'm done." We didn't say you don't learn. We suggest that you don't have to. You don't have to, but you do. What about *karma?* It's a choice, a self-determined and self-imposed choice.

Anonymous Question, Evening with Lazaris, Seattle, 1987

Death

Q: Lazaris,
would you
talk to us
about death
— and can
you program
to avoid cer-
tain realities,
like the death
of one's
parents and
oneself?

Lazaris: What about death? The real statement — assumption — behind this question is: Death is bad. And we would ask: Why? What's wrong with dying? Well, we're going to talk about some of the problems with dying, but we would ask: What's wrong with it? You see, you've been geared, you've been conditioned, to believe that it's bad, that death is a failure, that if you die you somehow have failed — unless you live to be ... well, very, very old. Even then, people treat it as a failure. "Oh, that's too bad." Why? What's so bad about it?

The world that you go into, the reality that you move into is far more exciting, we dare say, far more thrilling and far more to your liking than the one you're dealing with now. Death is something that you do, not because you have to, but because you decided to.

Your body is a vehicle. That's all it is. It's an illusion. It's made up of light and sound that is dense enough to be called a body.

When you watch television you see light and sound, and it looks like bodies walking around in your television screen. They aren't bodies. You know that. When you go to the movies and see figures on the big screen, they look like bodies moving around, too, but you know they're not. You know that's light and sound in coordination to create the illusion.

Well, you're just a three-dimensional illusion, and that body of yours is a vehicle. Now how would you feel about getting an automobile assigned to you at birth, but you could never get rid of it? You had to keep that same automobile ... from birth!? Well, even at 16, yes? Think back to the first automobile you had. How would you feel about still having to drive that? ... {laughter} ... "You mean I don't get to trade this one in?" No! You have to keep it, and you have to treat it right, and you have to program it to run forever. Would you like that? "No, I want to trade it in. I want a newer model!" Some of you trade them in every two years regardless. Some of you keep them a little longer if you particularly like them, but you always look forward to the new automobile — the new vehicle.

Well, similarly, death is a process of turning in the vehicle, and saying, "I'm done with this vehicle. I'm ready either to move on without a vehicle or to get another one." So indeed to program not to die? We would suggest: look deeper. Why are you considering death a failure? Why are you considering it bad and wrong? Why are you seeing it as something you never want to do?

Admittedly, you might not want to do it now or next week or next year or whatever, but sometime you're going to want to. You can program to be healthy and to live as long as you desire, to live to be as old as you desire to be, but eventually indeed you will want to die and be ready to die and be eager to do so. Truthfully, it is not inevitable as a "rule" or a "law," but it is something you will desire ... someday.

Also, there is the power of belief. You have been so conditioned to believe that you have to die at a certain age. Some people have a belief that they're going to die at 50 because their mother, father, brother and sister all died at age 50, "so I'm going to die at age 50." And many times they do. Others feel that "once I retire and the old ticker stops working so well, you know, there's not much use in living."

"You see, you've been geared, you've been conditioned, to believe that it's bad, that death is a failure, that if you die you somehow have failed."

Some of you who are led totally by your second *chakra* decide that once you can't have sex there's no reason to live, and therefore you go about the process of dying.

You've been conditioned to believe that the moment you're born you begin to die. What a devastating thought, but nonetheless ... So there are very high thresholds, and if you really wanted to get over it, you could. Ultimately, you don't really want to get over that threshold. You will want to die sometime. Eventually you — everyone — will choose to die.

Anonymous Question, Evening with Lazaris, Atlanta, 1987

Q: Death. Speak to us of physical death.

Lazaris: Well, it's a rather interesting concept, you know. You've been so afraid of it, and we understand that, certainly so. We understand your fears. We've heard you echo them. We've heard your call. But we would suggest that, in fact, death ultimately is the healer, as it is the ultimate end of your pain, the ultimate end of your fear, the ultimate end of your frustration in life. We do not encourage you to do it quickly. We do not encourage you to bring it on any sooner than you are fully willing to. But we would suggest that there will come a time, indeed, when each of you will choose to discard this form that you carry.

That discarding is the process called death. Some choose to do it with their eyes closed and pretend they can't see what's going on. Others choose to do it with their eyes open, and therefore more consciously select their death.

When you do decide to die — by whatever means, early or late in your life — what happens is you slip out of your body, much as you would slip out of a garment at night, and let it fall to the ground and seem lifeless around you. But you, you as the spark that you are, are still alive, still vibrant, still reaching. What do you see before you?

What? A most glorious light, a most glorious light, and that light attracts you, and that light draws you to it, and you want to reach for that light. You stretch for it, and at a certain point as you are reaching, it draws you in. As you are drawn, you realize how much you are loved by God, by God/Goddess/All That Is, and how capable you are of loving. It is toward this love, this love, this love and light that is God, that you are so drawn.

Lazaris: Oh, most definitely you do. After you go through the light, and have this most glorious of celebrations, most definitely you take a bit of a rest, you know? You carry forth with you much of your physical desire, and therefore bodies turn younger and thinner and more athletic and you get, finally, the body that you've always wanted, for a bit of time at least.

Q: Do we have the physical chance to come back?

You go into this wondrous somnambulistic state, half-awake, half-asleep. When you awaken, you look at your life, and you look it over, and review it, to see what you've done and what you've accomplished — not in a judgmental way, not in a harsh way, but just in an evaluative way.

Then you decide. You see, this power of choice is effective not only in your physical world, but in the world beyond. You decide: Do you want to come back into a physical form or do you not? Are you most suited to learn by reentering this density that you call physicalness, or are you most suited to learn without it?

The choice very clearly is yours, absolutely. There is no referee; there's no judge. There's no one there saying, "Ah ..." No. You are the one who decides. At times it would seem almost better if someone else did make those choices and decisions, because you are much harsher on yourself than anyone else would be. However, it is always you who chooses and decides.

Merv Griffin, The Merv Griffin Show, July, 1986

Q: You've described the death experience as passing through a tunnel with the sound of wind rushing in our ears. What happens when you emerge from the tunnel?

Lazaris: Wonderful things! What happens when you die? Well, let's not belabor it, because we have talked about it frequently. When you die you leave your body — you leave your body behind. You go out of body, and it is a terrifying experience because you *believe* it is, because you've been conditioned to believe it is, because you get close to that brink, and you get scared. What if it's not there? What if there isn't a heaven? What if there isn't a God? What if the existentialists are right, and your body just rots in the ground, and you go into some sort of oblivion?

Nonetheless, you have all these sorts of resistances right at the edge. Therefore, you sort of faint when you leave your body. ... {laughter} ... It's a trauma, you know?

You're born in trauma, and you die in trauma, many of you. When you're born, you're amazed that you're confined to this tiny body that doesn't even work! ...

{laughter} ... And you wonder, "Did I sign up for this?" ... {laughter} ...

Then you make it work. "All right, if this is what I have, I'd better roll up the old sleeves here and get this body to grow and to function and to be able to walk and talk and do both those things all at the same time!" Then you go on and do other things more sophisticatedly. Then you reach that point of death when you're finally going to be liberated from this body, and you say, "Whoa! Wait a minute! Do I really have to be free of it?"

So when you die, many people "faint." It just sort of goes to black, yes? Well, very quickly you revive. It lasts whatever length of Earth time. It's outside of time by that point. But then you revive, and you are drawn to a tunnel of light, clearly so.

At the other end of that tunnel is everybody you want to have be there ... all the relatives whom you miss, the ones who died before you ... none of the ones you don't care for. ... {laughter} ... And since consciousness is multi-dimensional, all those people who are still alive that you would like to have there are there, also. So your kids, your friends, all the ones you left behind are there. It's a huge celebration, a huge party!

Now some who have a very Fundamentalist belief and have fears of maybe going to hell will take a little sidestep, and they'll go sliding down toward hell, you see? They'll get right to the edge, and they'll teeter on the edge, but alas, nobody ever goes! ... {laughter} ... Some Fundamentalists get very close ... {laughter} ... not because they belong there, but because they're so afraid of it that they come right up to the edge and: "Whoa! I looked into hell! And I saw the Devil looking back at me! And I commanded the Devil to get out!" So they have their feared brush with the Devil, and then they go through the light into heaven, where they knew they belonged all along. ... {laughter} ...

So you go into heaven. You go into this wonderful place that is this huge celebration with everybody you want to be there ... including historical people you always wanted to meet. Everyone is there coming up to greet you.

You go through this grand celebration, and then you go to sleep. You go into a somnambulistic state that can last in Earth time a few minutes, a few hours, a few years, a few decades. It is like that wondrous period when you wake up in the morning and you get to sleep that extra half-hour — the time when you are half-awake and half-asleep, where you can just snuggle in when it's chilly, or listen to the birds chirp when it's a beautiful morning. You enter a somnambulism, a floating, wondrous state.

Then you wake up, and you experience the heaven you anticipated. If you thought that heaven was streets paved with gold, then you'll find a city with streets paved with gold, angels with harps, and wondrous creatures of this sort, and you'll play "Heaven" for awhile.

"It's rather beautiful, it's rather wonderful, and it's the ultimate healing. It's important perhaps to remember that. Death is the ultimate healing."

At a certain point you say, "Is this all there is?" Then the walls fall down, and you get down to the serious work of growing, of reviewing the life you experienced, of putting it in context to the other lifetimes you've experienced, of going to classes. You talk to friends, you get involved in activities, you do all kinds of things in your process of reviewing.

Ultimately you make another decision: Do I want to go back into the physical? Do I want to pick another lifetime? There's a broad array of them out there. You decide: "I want to learn this. I want to learn that. I want to deal with this, that and the other. That one will do.

That lifetime. I'll take that one." Then you'll create and put the arrangements together to thus reenter into physical incarnation.

Or you'll decide: "No, I'm done. I don't need to do any more physical lifetimes. I'm not done growing, but I've learned everything that I can learn or want to learn from the Physical Plane." Two statements: can learn and want to learn. "So I'm going to do my growth without body now, and therefore I'm going to move on."

That's what the death experience is like. It's rather beautiful, it's rather wonderful, and it's the ultimate healing. It's important perhaps to remember that. Death is the ultimate healing. It ends the physical misery. It ends the physical limitation.

*"There is a way to transcend death, however, and that way — the adult way, as we call it — is to consciously die, to **consciously** die."*

Can you "learn to transcend death?" Can you be immortal? Now there are two approaches to immortality. One approach, which we would plainly say is rather adolescent, is the approach to immortality which says you've got to keep the same body you have. "I want to live to be 200, 300 — I want to live forever in this body." Why on Earth would you want to? Why? We are rather amazed by that, just as we are by why you might want to keep the same automobile forever and ever. But we would suggest here some people are attempting that, and quite frankly they won't succeed. Quite frankly, their belief structures, the importance of giving up the body, and the value of being detached from it are such that they won't ever succeed at that kind of immortality.

Oh yes, human consciousness is going to be able to live to be 100, 120, 130 years old. That's not going to be a difficulty in a number of years. Out of a lot of the diseases that are currently operative, one of the by-products is going to be a tremendous knowledge of longevity, such that people will be able to live to be

100, 120, or 130 — and not by replacing all their organs. More and more people will be living to be that age. That is much more viable, much more possible — but not to live forever.

There is a way to transcend, however, and that way — the adult way, as we call it — is to consciously die, to *consciously* die. You know, we take you on meditations, right? In those meditations you close your eyes, and you relax, and you lift yourself out of your body. Sometimes you float up and out, and you go here or there.

Well, immortality, in the truest sense of the word, can be accomplished. You can decide "today's a good day to die," and lie down and close your eyes. You enter a "meditation," and your light body stands up, fully conscious, climbs out of your body, and leaves it for good. Now that, we would suggest, is true immortality, where you "never die," where you never die, because you are fully conscious throughout the entire experience.

The movie *Cocoon* is a movie that appeals to a lot of people because they came close (they didn't really quite do that, but they came close) to portraying conscious death, immortality, when all these old people decided, and together, at one time, sort of ascended, yes? You can approach death by deciding, "Today is a good day to die, and, therefore, I'm going to go to bed tonight, and I'm going to consciously die."

You can decide not to "faint."

Anonymous Question, Evening with Lazaris, Atlanta, 1987

Lazaris: Yes, it is important. Obviously, we do talk primarily about the person who is dying because that's rather final, in that regard, for many of you, and it's important to want to know about it.

Q: Most of your comments on death seem to be directed toward the one who is dying. Can you offer some insights to the ones who are left here to deal with this phenomenon?

For those who remain, what's important is realizing why you are sad. You know, we tell you it's beautiful, it's wonderful, it's a huge party, you experience heaven, no one ever goes to hell, no one ever has a bad time, it's always wonderful, and you learn, and you grow, and it's wonderful — it's fantastic! It's being able to program your reality and get it every time. That's what you're shooting for here, right?

You are not sad when *you* die. Why would you be sad when *they* die? Because you're going to miss the person. You're not really sad they're dying as much as you're sad they're leaving.

You think about a friend. You've had a lifelong friend, and they come and announce that they're moving to Hong Kong. You're going to be sad. Now imagine they say, "I'm going to move to Hong Kong, and I'm never going to write, I'm never going to telephone, and you'll never see me again." Of course you're going to be very sad.

Death is an intensification of that, an exponential of that, because they're going away. From your perspective they're never going to come back. You're not absolutely sure where or to what they are going.

You can hear our words, but, hey, you've kind of got to experience it to know it's real. And what if we're wrong? That's more than sad. That's scary.

And so when someone dies, there is a natural sense of loss, a natural sense of missing them. You're not really mourning that they are dead. You're mourning that you are alone, that you got left behind.

We would also suggest that many times you're angry. "How dare they leave me! How dare they leave me!" Particularly a loved one. You're married to someone, or you've been with someone for lots of years as a friend, as a partner, and they up and left. They didn't consult you. They just did it on their own, and you're angry.

But, you see, you're not supposed to be angry. You wonder: "Isn't that a terrible thing to say? I'm so angry at them for dying. Oh, that's terrible!" So, therefore, you convert it into another feeling. You feel guilty, you feel bad, you feel this wave of unidentified feeling.

*"When some-
one dies, feel
the full range
of emotion, and
let yourself feel
that full range
as intensely as
you can ...
Don't be 'big'
about it. Be
emotional
about it!"*

What's important around death is to realize that no matter how much you understand what it's like, you are going to feel sad. Don't deny your feeling. No matter how much you understand it, you are going to be angry, just as you'd be angry at a friend who applied for a transfer and is going to move thousands of miles away without telling you. You go over to their house one day and they're gone, or they're packing, on the way out the door. There's nothing you can do to stop it.

You're going to be angry. You're going to feel hurt. You're going to feel betrayed. You're going to feel fear.

The thing that is important for the living: When someone dies, let yourself mourn. Don't do a metaphysical "better than": "Well, I know what death is like, and I know this, and I know that, and I'm not going to mourn." Mourn. Cry. Wail. Thrash about. Get angry. Get hurt. Feel the betrayal. Feel the sadness. Feel the hurt. Feel the remorse. Feel the loss and the loneliness. Feel it, and feel it intensely. Don't drag it out. Don't spend a year or two. Feel it intensely. Don't hold yourself back. When you can feel it intensely, you can release it. You can release it.

If you feel it in a mediocre way, then you'll drag it out, and when you think you're past it, it'll bubble up again, and you'll feel it all over again. It can go on for years and years and years. If you refuse to feel it at all ... "I refuse to deal with it" ... you have to numb yourself out. Therefore, you shut down, and you will shut down other parts of yourself as well.

When someone dies, feel the full range of emotion, and let yourself feel that full range as intensely as you can. Take a day off from work if you need to. Take some time away. Don't be "big" about it. Be emotional about it!

Recently a dear friend of the staff, in fact someone on the staff, had an auto accident. The staff realized that she could well have been killed. In fact, when one looks at the automobile, it's amazing, it's truly a miracle that she wasn't. She came out with six broken ribs. That's all. More damage was done at the hospital than in the accident, as a matter of fact. ... {laughter} ...

But it hit everybody: She could have died. As metaphysical as everybody is, that realization was a real scary and very sad thought. Everybody knows that when people do start dying eventually — and they're going to — that it's going to be something very difficult to deal with.

But the way to deal with it is to feel it. Feel it. All the range of it. You're going to be angry at God for taking them. You're going to be angry at a world for whatever they died of. You want to strike out at that world. Well, do it in a way that's appropriate. Feel it as intensely and as fully as you possibly can, for that's how you get it out of you and release it.

Be done with it. Then when it's all done, you can sit around and talk more philosophically about what's it like to be dead.

We deal with a lot of people who obviously are dealing with death. We deal with a lot of people dying. We tell them what it's like and describe it to them, and we are there for them if they so desire, and work with them over the hump, as it were.

It is a sadness, there's no question, because you're lonely and left behind, and that's sad. So understand what you're really mourning. You're mourning your loss, not their gain. If you can put it in that perspective, it is much easier to deal with.

Anonymous Question, Evening with Lazaris, Atlanta, 1987

With love and peace ...

Lazaris

The Future & Its Vision

The Doomsayers & Predictions of the Future — Earth Changes
Dealing with Fears of the Future — The Environment: Its Survival
The Positive Future — Dreaming the Future — Why Dream?

The Doomsayers &
Predictions of the Future

"The problem is not that the world is going to come to an end, but that the world isn't going to come to an end, and you're all still going to be here, needing to solve all those problems."

Q: What is your opinion of the doomsayers, those who prophesy terrible catastrophes?

Lazaris: We feel a certain sadness for their limited thought. Those who are so quick to predict doom look at the world and say, "My goodness. There's pollution. There are nuclear difficulties ... I don't know how to solve that. I can't imagine any solution to any of these problems. The only thing I can think of is that it's all going to be destroyed. So therefore, I am going to predict that destruction. Because I can't see a solution, there is no solution."

If it doesn't happen, everyone is going to be so happy that they aren't going to pay attention to the fact that the predictions were wrong. Therefore, there is a certain safety in predicting doom.

Many now who are predicting those things are simply revealing their own limited thought, their inability to realize that just because they don't have any solutions doesn't mean the solutions do not exist. It doesn't mean somebody else doesn't have solutions.

There is a certain egocentricity in this limited thought. There is an arrogance.

Similarly, they look at their metaphysics as a popularity contest, and their "spiritual following" as validation and confirmation of their "spiritual teachings." Political dictators and religious zealots always warned of impending doom to engender followers and control people: "If you don't do as I tell you, the whole world is going to be destroyed — and primarily *you* will be destroyed!" Unfortunately, those tactics have never changed.

If you believe and feel that there are these destructions, certainly you can prove yourself correct. If you feel it, and you think it, and you look for it, you are going to generate it.

But instead, you can say, "No. I am the creator of *my* reality, and I refuse to create *those* realities. Instead, I'm going to create the realities where somebody comes up with solutions, where somebody finds the answers to solve these particular problems. Just because I can't see or find the solutions doesn't mean solutions aren't out there somewhere."

You can choose to live in a reality where the future is glorious, where the future is there. The problem is not that the world is going to come to an end, but that the world isn't going to come to an end, and you're all still going to be here, needing to solve all those problems.

*Alan Vaughan, **Whole Life Monthly**, Santa Monica*

Q: Lazaris, in both the Christian and metaphysical communities there seem to be very dire predictions of the future. What do these predictions mean, and how can we understand them, knowing also that we create our own reality completely?

Lazaris: There has always been curiosity about predictions of the future. Despite the vast diversity of humankind, throughout the entirety of the world, there has always been sort of an eerie hush whenever the soothsayer or the oracle was about to speak. Whether these predictions ushered forth came from the misfit or the mystic, you stopped, you listened, intrigued.

As this century comes to a close, the interest and the curiosity is the same as it always has been. It differs, however, because you are a participant this time. The interest and the curiosity, which has objectively belonged to humanity, now is yours.

It also differs because there are so many varying sources of prediction, and so many drawing what appear, at least, to be similar conclusions.

To look more closely, we must examine two groups of predictions: those offered by the serious seers and those presented by the circus of seers who think they have found a bandwagon upon which to hop.

Of the latter group, from the Fundamentalist spirituality of Christianity to the alternative spirituality of metaphysics, there are those who have stooped to manipulate you with fear. They often honestly do not understand, fully believe, or even begin to know what they are teaching. Therefore, they must resort to fear tactics to gain support and popularity. They often privately devalue themselves so much that they project their own sense of worthlessness and their own lack of self-respect onto humanity. Therefore, it becomes all right with them to trade on humanity's vulnerability at the expense and consequence of their own. Sadly, it works. Fortunately, not for long.

Within each of you there lies a well of fear. The fear that initially began with a fear of loneliness and aloneness, a fear of being cut off, of being separate, a fear of alienation and disenfranchisement, a fear of disorder and of failure — this well of fear is something you carry with you. It expresses itself in a variety of ways from anxiety, perhaps the most nebulous form, to paranoia, the most rigid form. You are constantly dealing with releasing fear.

To tap into this well with the intention of releasing it is called growth. To tap into this well with the intention of controlling the human spirit is called manipulation.

It is truly unconscionable for anyone to resort to manipulations of fear, to twist and to turn that fear for their own selfish ends. It is most particularly unconscionable for anyone in the field of human potential, metaphysics, and/or spirituality to stoop so very low.

Though unconscionable, there are those who are doing it. Most particularly now, at the close of the century, at a time when many are speaking of an end of an Old Age and a beginning of a New Age, there is the circus of seers who are trying to play with you.

However, there are also those who, quite legitimately, are offering their predictions, and these predictions may similarly seem very dire. Most notable among these legitimate seers are the likes of Nostradamus and his predictions, Eastern *yugas* and their descriptions and depictions, the Mayan Calendar, the Pyramid of Cheops, the Hopi Calendar, Yeats and his poetic outline of the future of humanity, and the *Book of Revelation* and its similarly poetic, but quite different, predictions of the "end times." All these systems have four things in common:

First: All the major predictions of each were made hundreds or even thousands of years ago.

Second: Each of the systems has demonstrated a certain degree of eerie and uncanny accuracy, particularly

"Within each of you there lies a well of fear ... To tap into this well with the intention of releasing it is called growth. To tap into this well with the intention of controlling the human spirit is called manipulation."

when the predictions have been interpreted in retrospect.

Third: All of the systems depict a breakdown of the consensus reality.

Fourth: They all stop. They all end their predictions at or about the time of the year 2000.

These four similarities have been used by many to suggest that all these systems are accurately depicting the end of humanity.

First, they have used the fact that all these predictions occurred hundreds and even thousands of years ago as an indication of the prowess and the accuracy — specifically, the psychic accuracy — of the predictors.

Secondly, because so many predictions have been uncannily accurate, particularly when interpreted in retrospect, they assume that those which have not yet occurred or have not yet been interpreted, will happen in a matter of time. Therefore, they suggest that all the predictions will ultimately prove to be accurate.

Because of these first two considerations, the third commonality — depiction of a breakdown of the consensus reality — is assumed to be true as well.

Finally, because the predictions stop at or about the year 2000, the conclusion is drawn that those wise seers knew the world was coming to an end at that same time.

These conclusions are understandable, but that they are understandable does not make them correct. We would suggest an alternative set of conclusions to be drawn from these four points of commonality:

First: The predictions were made hundreds and even thousands of years ago at a time when the seat of power, the seat of consciousness, within each human being rested securely in the subconscious self.

Those predictors and depictors, so many hundreds and thousands of years ago, operated at a time when you as a humanity were willing to allow your reality to be dictated by your subconscious mind. Therefore, the seers could accurately predict a future that was subconsciously determined and subconsciously destined to be.

At this timing of the late 1900s moving into the years 2000, the seat of power, the seat of determining your future, lies no longer in your subconscious mind, but rather lies, more and more, in your conscious mind, where you have choice, where you have the power of choosing the future and the reality you want to create.

We suggest that those same seers, if they were existing today, because your reality is now created consciously, would not be so presumptuous as to make such predictions as they did so many hundreds, even thousands, of years ago.

Second: The interpretations are so seemingly uncannily accurate, particularly in retrospect, for two reasons:

First, because they were made at a time when the seat of power was located in the subconscious self, the predictions were more accurate. The timings of wars, beginnings and endings, the timing of major changes of human consciousness, the timing of new directions of growth were indeed quite able to be predicted at a time when power was located more automatically within the subconscious self.

Secondly, predictions are interpreted so accurately in retrospect because they are so often written poetically. One of the measures of truly powerful poetry is that it can take the general journey of humanity and make it seem as though it is your own, and it can take the personal journey of one and make it seem as though it's true for everyone. Because the predictions have been written poetically, they are often a reflection of one's

"Those who were so wise and so insightful as to be able to make predictions that would come true hundreds, indeed thousands, of years later ... also understood that there would be a time when you would take your power back, when you would not allow others to tell you what your future would be ..."

personal journey and a reflection of the larger, symbolic journey of all of humanity.

Third: As you move from that which is called the Old Age into that which is called the New Age — as you move from what is more accurately referred to as the Old Spirituality into that which is more correctly the New Spirituality — there will be a breakdown of the consensus reality. When a world that has been seen as being totally objective is proved to be subjective — when a world which hitherto has been called subjective all of a sudden becomes very objective — then the world will indeed seem very topsy-turvy. The consensus indeed will seem to have come to an end.

There will be those who face such a reality and decide they cannot deal with it, and therefore choose in their own way to bring it to an end personally and collectively. There will be others, such as those of you who are growing, truly growing spiritually, who will see this not as a time of end, but indeed as a time of beginning — a time when the consensus reality will indeed die, but will also indeed give birth to a new reality, to a New Spirituality, to a new dawn, to a New Age.

Finally: The predictions do stop — that is correct — but they stop not because the world is coming to an end, but rather because the Old Age is giving way to the New. The old world is about to give birth to a New Age of Spirituality.

You see, those who were so wise and so insightful as to be able to make predictions that would come true hundreds, indeed thousands, of years later — those that had that kind of insight, that kind of wisdom, that kind of understanding — also understood the New Age, also understood that there would be a time when you would take your power back, when you would not allow others to tell you what your future would be, when you would decide that you are the master and determiner of

> *"... all the calendars, the markings in pyramids, all the poetry from Nostradamus, from the Eastern mystics, from Yeats, and the revelatory statements of the Bible depict a personal journey. They depict a personal change, a personal growth, and stop — not because the world ends, but because life truly begins."*

your destiny, when you would empower yourself so as to stop looking for destiny and start creating it.

Those that were so insightful understood that there would be a time when you would love yourself enough to love someone else, when you would love yourself enough to love something and someone that was more than you. They understood there would be a time when you would value yourself, when you would both recognize and accept that value personally and collectively.

They understood that there would be a time when you would let your past die to you, to give birth to a future. They knew that you would be able to recognize a living, breathing, loving, embracing God/Goddess/ All That Is that would be a part of you. They knew that there was a time that would come when you would stop looking for and start choosing your destiny — stop waiting for others to give it to you and start choosing it for yourself. They knew there would be a time when you would not give up your will, but that you would accept your will *and* the will of God/Goddess/All That Is in a co-creating capacity. They knew there would be a time when you would merge your will with that of a higher force. They knew that there would be this age that was new. They would not be so presumptuous to presume, so limited as to predict, what *you* would create.

No, all the calendars, the markings in pyramids, all the poetry from Nostradamus, from the Eastern mystics, from Yeats, and the revelatory statements of the Bible depict a personal journey. They depict a personal change, a personal growth, and stop — not because the world ends, but because life truly begins.

Always remember: You create your own reality. There is no fine print. There is no asterisk. You create it all.

*Paul Zuromski, **Body, Mind & Spirit**, Johnston, Rhode Island*

Q: Dooms-
dayers. You
know as well
as I there's
quite a few of
them out
there!

Lazaris: Oh,
aren't there
though!

Q: Many of
them predict
horrendous
Earth chan-
ges. I don't
agree with
them. I know
you don't
agree with
them.

Lazaris: Yes.
Exactly.

Q: But it's
very interest-
ing just to
note that in
the past few
weeks (Oc-
tober, 1987)
that they talk
about a huge
hole in the
ozone layer ...
And, of
course, in
California
they just had
a little bit of
rippling, and
they're wait-
ing for the
"Big One."

Lazaris: Well, indeed there is a hole in the ozone. At the South Pole, the Antarctic area, it's very thin, and in the month of October it's particularly thinner than ever. Yes, it is a very real concern. Pollution of the atmosphere from various flourocarbons, and various other by-products of industry, has had a very damaging and a continuously damaging effect on that ozone layer, there is no question.

However, the attitude that therefore there is no hope is wrong. Damage has been done, there's no question. To date there is no complete solution to rebuilding an ozone layer, that's for sure. But there are progresses being made within industry and within the particular groups of people fighting pollution. They are making headway, both to reduce significantly those factors that adversely affect that ozone layer and to begin to rebuild it.

In time there will be solutions. Not within the next five years, but by the turn of the century there are very real possibilities that there will be solutions, ways in which not only can you eliminate those detriments to that ozone layer, but also you can actually work to improve the layer itself. Those solutions have not been truly dreamt yet.

It is not our place to tell you, "This is the formula. This is the solution. This is where to look. This is the future professor that's going to come up with the answer." No, it is your reality; it is your world to fix and to make work. Solutions will be found. Solutions will be dreamt.

There was a (Richter Magnitude) 5.9 earthquake in California, and there were several people who were killed in that process. For them that was the "Big One." We suggest here that, absolutely, for those particular individuals, that earthquake was the one that destroyed

California and destroyed their life. For you physical beings it's tragic to lose any life at all.

At the same time there was an unseasonable snowstorm in New York State. How many people died in that? There were about twice as many as died in the earthquake.

There are those who *want* to look and say, "Oh, my gosh! See, I knew it. Look at California. They had an earthquake, and it killed several people. It's just the beginning." But in upstate New York you had a snowstorm that killed twice as many, and people ignore that, saying, "But, oh, that's not part of our Doom and Gloom." Those people are just as dead, and the tragedy is just as tragic. The earthquake in California is not evidence of the end of the world.

Look at the positive side. What could have been a disaster with hundreds of thousands of people potentially killed turned out to be a minimal disaster that only cost money, which can be artificially recreated, and a few lives which were unfortunately and tragically lost. It's a matter of: What do you want to see? People who want to see Doom and Gloom can find it. People who want to see Hope and Prosperity can find that as well. It's up to each individual to decide which they want to create, for the world will provide ample opportunity to have whatever you want.

How many people died in heat waves this last summer? No one pays attention to them, as though somehow they don't count, somehow that doesn't matter because it's not part of the grand scheme of destruction of those who are ... selling fear. There are some who hear of tragedy and disaster and are almost delighted: "Oh goody, it happened, and oh, goody, people died. I was right!" It's really sad.

"What do you want to see? People who want to see Doom and Gloom can find it. People who want to see Hope and Prosperity can find that as well. It's up to each individual to decide ..."

We know that everybody who talks about Doom and Gloom is not of that camp, clearly not, but there are those within that group that are absolutely delighted to see and hear that their "predictions" might well be coming true. There's a sad twist of events there that seems somehow unfortunate, yes?

*Paul Zuromski, **Body, Mind & Spirit**, Johnston, Rhode Island*

Earth Changes

Q: Lazaris, will you talk about Earth changes?

Lazaris: Well, in November of 1986 we went into that in great depth. We also recorded a video tape. We were hesitant to do that even then because each person creates their own reality.

It's always fascinating to us as people get involved in metaphysics and discover that concept: "I create my own reality. Everyone creates their own reality. It's so liberating, so free, so wonderful!" Then they turn around and say, "And when is the earthquake going to come?" Now wait a moment! If you create your own reality, which you do and which now even you are saying you do, then *you* decide when the earthquake is going to come. You don't need to ask us. You decide. When is it? You had one down there (in the San Diego area) in 1986. You don't often have them down there. Somebody must have slipped up a bit.

So to the first, the Earth changes are going to be the changes you expect. We don't mean you as a mass of humanity. We mean you as an individual. There are those who are absolutely convinced of it: "I know it! I know it! I'll die in an earthquake! I know it is going to happen. I'll be sound asleep, and my house is going collapse around me, and I'll die!" They just absolutely *know* that truth for themselves, and we suggest: That's their truth. That's their reality, and undoubtedly they can create that. Does that mean if they live in San Diego that they'd create it for all San Diego? No. They would create their particular set, their quite unique reality, of having this happen to them.

Other people are absolutely convinced: "No way is an earthquake going to attack me. No way am I going to be anywhere near one of those things." And we suggest they always manage to avoid it. So, to one extent the Earth changes are going to be quite personalized. Each individual will have them.

But we understand, indeed, that there are many now who are speaking of these changes. From the very Fundamentalist Christians to the very reactionary metaphysicians, many are talking of all the devastating things that are going to be happening. A lot of people are getting very frightened.

It's rather intriguing, in that sense, you know. Some people don't want to hear that everything can be fine. You go to hear a talk, and someone tells you about how terrible things are going to be: "There are going to be earthquakes and pollution and droughts and people killing each other. The water and the air are going to be poisoned. There's going to be nuclear waste just lying around on the ground, and it's all going to be for naught."

But, you know, if you listen to all that, although it is as scary as it can be, there's also something very intriguing there, because then you don't have to think about how you're going to make the mortgage payment, what you're going to do about your teenage son on drugs, or what you're going to do about your older daughter who's getting a divorce and who's going to keep the kids — "I don't want them, but I'll take them if I have

"... the Earth changes are going to be the changes you expect. We don't mean you as a mass of humanity. We mean you as an individual."

to." You don't know what you're going to do about this relationship you're in. It's not really what you want, but you don't want to get rid of it. You don't like thinking about those problems.

You've been thinking about those problems for years, and now you can think about how you're going to survive. Are you going to have enough water? Are you going to dig a well? Are you going to get your chicken and your cow and go live in the country? And so, there's a certain romantic quality to hearing about all this destruction. Therefore, to hear, "Hey, it doesn't have to be that way — it can be different than that ..." You respond: "You mean then I've got to go back to thinking about all those mundane problems that aren't as romantic and aren't as much fun?" So people don't always like to hear that everything can be fine.

Because of the amount of energy involved with this issue we decided to do a video tape and a weekend activity in November of 1986 called *Changing: The Future Vision*. We wanted to talk about some of the changes that would occur, and more importantly we wanted to talk about what you could do about it ... how you can change those changes, how you can change the course of the future. Yes, there will be earthquakes in California. It doesn't take much of a psychic or much of a mystic to tell you that. There have been earthquakes in California for as long as there's been a California!

We would suggest here that over the next several years there will be certain major earthquakes that will occur, and there will, unfortunately, be a loss of life — but not a loss of California. Individuals who, quite frankly, have chosen for their own personal reasons to exit their physical incarnation, will manage to be at the right place at the right time to make that exit. This again is geological, and not awfully mystical. But those changes will not be as severe, nor as damaging, as many would like to convince themselves — and would like to convince you.

There will be more natural kinds of "disasters," but again they will be limited. The losses will be, perhaps, astronomical in terms of dollars and cents, but they will be amazingly minimal in terms of the number of people who might be lost or who might be destroyed in such activities. We want to teach people what to do to prevent disasters from happening. We want to show you how to make sure that these disturbing realities don't occur: "This is the time to begin programming. This is how to go about it."

We would refer, for example, to the Southeast situation, the drought that occurred there. Many of those who were so eager to look for destruction, so eager to find a solutionless reality, pointed their fingers and said, "See, it's beginning. See, the drought is the worst it's ever been. See, this is the beginning of the end." They pointed a finger, but they didn't lift a finger. They pointed in blame, and some, in their righteousness, said, "See, I told you so."

Other people lifted a finger to help. Other people loved. Other people said, "Yes, here's a problem. Let's do something about it." Farmers in the Midwest packed up their hay. It didn't require a governmental decision. It didn't require a bureaucratic decision. It took one man watching his CNN News to say, "I'm going to do something about this." And he took action, and others followed suit. They sent hay.

Others, metaphysicians, who aren't so convinced that the world is going to be destroyed and aren't so convinced that they don't have any impact, started programming. They started visualizing, started sending love and energy and sending emotion. Emotion, feeling. That's what water is, after all. They sent feeling to this area that was drying up, to this area where the emo-

"It is in this particular attitude that we see the real danger: Knowing that there's going to be something go wrong, you don't even begin looking for a solution. You get caught up in believing the negativity is inevitable, rather than looking for the possibility of changing it."

tions were drying up. They were sending love, sending water, sending energy in their minds.

And it began to rain, and it began to rain despite the meteorological decision at the beginning of August, 1986, that said, "There's no relief in sight for the entire months of August and September. At best, maybe in October there might be some rain." But it rained in August, and it rained, and it rained, and the drought was over. Some, with lackluster enthusiasm said, "Well, gee, that's great. That's wonderful." It's almost as if some people were disappointed: "Oh, that wasn't the beginning of the end. Gee, I wonder when it's going to happen."

It is in this particular attitude that we see the real danger: Knowing that there's going to be something go wrong, you don't even begin looking for a solution. You get caught up in believing the negativity is inevitable, rather than looking for the possibility of changing it.

Many years ago in your world, before there were civilizations, there were cataclysmic changes, most definitely. Your scientists tell you of the huge mastodons that are found with flowers in their mouths, frozen in the snow, etc. You know from your geological lookings at the Earth, and from the fossil testings, that there were dramatic cataclysmic changes in the Earth's reality. But the thing that's different is that there are now people on your planet, spiritual people, who love, people who care, people who have power to create their own reality.

We suggested this to someone once, and they said, "Yes, but the Earth doesn't care. The Earth has to change, and the Earth doesn't care about people." Maybe the Earth doesn't, although we suggest, in fact, that the Earth does care, but even beyond that, God cares. God/Goddess/All That Is cares and people care ... and people care.

You see, the drought in the Southeast could have gone on, we suppose, through August and all of September, and indeed people could have been clicking their tongues and saying, "Tsk, tsk, what a tragedy ... what a pity." But some — enough — people loved. People cared. People did something. People took action. Well, that didn't happen billions of years ago when there weren't people here, but it is happening now. And that's a factor that negative, cynical and limited people don't want to admit.

You have impact. Your decision, what you want in your reality, matters and does make a difference. Therefore, those types of cataclysmic changes that happened billions of years ago "cannot happen now" because there are people, because you care, because you love, because you can decide, "No, I don't want that reality." You have impact. The factor of human impact and the factor of a new level of spirituality that is operative in your country and in your world are factors that those doomsdayists never took into account.

Whether you are metaphysical or whether you are Fundamentalist, there is an earnest desire for God. You will do almost anything to find that God energy. You will listen to the most outlandish Fundamentalist Bible-thumping radical or reactionary Christian. You will listen to the most outlandish metaphysician, in that particular regard, too.

You don't necessarily believe that a consciousness is coming from the sixth dimension or the tenth dimension or from the dark side of the Moon, or whatever, but you are so eager to be spiritual, so eager to touch God, so eager to know that energy that you will overlook many of these obvious inconsistencies, just as Christians will overlook the rantings and ravings of righteousness in their own religion. You want to know

"You have impact. Your decision, what you want in your reality, matters and does make a difference. ... You have impact. The factor of human impact and the factor of a new level of spirituality that is operative in your country and in your world are factors that those doomsdayists never took into account."

God so much — you want to feel that sense of God so very much.

There's so much love in your country, in that sense, even among people who think they hate and even among people who treat each other in very hateful ways. Underneath it, if trouble comes, you aren't going to get shotguns and shoot each other. You are going to welcome each other. You are going to help each other. You are going to work to love each other. Because of your spiritual search, you will draw upon the best of the human condition. You will draw upon your loving nature.

In your world, on the whole Earth planet for that matter — it's not just limited to your country — the level of spirituality, the desire to grow, the desire to have a living, breathing, loving, embracing relationship with whatever you call God, Goddess, or All That Is, is so profoundly powerful.

The extraterrestrials that are supposedly here to help you are perhaps often here to learn from you. It is time for you to stop thinking that you are at the bottom of the garbage heap, to stop thinking that you're the "low-life" of the cosmos and that everything would be good if "you guys would just straighten up." Maybe those extraterrestrials who are here supposedly to teach you are, in fact, here to observe you, to learn from you, to expand *their* spirituality. Perhaps they are here to come closer to the level that you — even in your "ignorance," even in your unknowing state — have already accomplished.

People who can't begin to spell metaphysics and who think the *kundalini* is some sort of Italian sausage have more love and more desire to be happy than you realize. Start counting on the value of human consciousness. Start realizing you create your own reality.

Start realizing that *you*, not the doomsayers, will decide your future.

Patricia Clay, *Infinite Thought*, San Diego

Dealing with Fears
of the Future

Lazaris: First of all, in the larger sense, the answer to the worldwide fear of devastation lies basically in one word: Vision. People need to develop a vision, which is more than a dream. A dream is important. A dream is your desire, your expectation, and indeed your imagination, working toward the creation of your reality.

When a dream involves all your senses, when a dream is so vivid that the distinction between the dream and the reality blurs, the dream becomes a vision.

People need to have vision for themselves personally, and they also need to have vision for the world at large. Many of you are now doing that. We personally have talked with thousands of you directly about working with this whole concept of vision. Having vision has already had impact.

A number of the negative predictions that the naysayers are and were making are now turning around. They are *not* happening. Certain of those naysayers, not too long from now, are going to be retracting some of their negativity. Undoubtedly, excuses will be offered about how *they* changed it, and how *they* fixed it up. They will, however, be retracting some of their negativity.

Q: You also speak of the fact that there are so many of the naysayers. Could you talk about concrete steps to releasing the fears we all have about what they're saying? We hear things ...

Lazaris: It gets real scary.

Q: We have fears, yet I appreciate what you say that now, in this New Age, we can grow with joy and love. What can we do about the fear?

But in a personal sense, how do you deal with your personal fears? We suggest it's important, ironically, to know what fear is, and to understand what the bottom-line fear is.

The bottom-line fear is a fear of loneliness. Every fear that you have, no matter what it is — somebody in the closet who is going to jump out and attack you, or the fear that you're going to go broke, that you're going to get sick, that that little lump is going to turn out to be your end-all — no matter what the fear is, it always reduces down to the fear of loneliness. Therefore, when you feel fear, rather than playing around with it, running from it, and getting into the high drama of it, immediately stop and say, "Okay, what is the loneliness that I'm running from? What is the loneliness I'm running from?" And if you'll answer that question ...

Secondly, fear is also a response to a feeling that you don't love "good enough." The negativity in your life — all of it — reduces to that particular factor: "I'm afraid that I don't love good enough." You are so afraid that you don't love "good enough" that you spend most of your time covering up that fear.

Face that fear, no matter how mundane it may seem, and reduce it to the loneliness and to the feeling: "I don't think I love good enough." Then answer the fear: "What can I do to make sure I'm not lonely? What can I do to show myself that I do love good enough?" If you'll do that, we suggest, the fear can resolve itself.

"The bottom-line fear is a fear of loneliness. Every fear that you have, no matter what it is ... always reduces down to the fear of loneliness."

Thirdly, it is important to realize that you can play through your fear. We suggest that you can do what we call a "fear letter." It's a very specific technique. "Dear _____ (put your own name), I'm scared." And just write this letter, be it a paragraph or 20 pages, of free-flowing expression of your fear. "I'm scared of this. I'm scared of that." Detail it. Don't just say, "I'm afraid that something awful is going to happen." Rather say, "I'm afraid that I'm going to be driving down the highway, and a car is going to come veering at me, and we're going to smash into each other, and the steering wheel's going to impale me, and I'm not going to die right away, and I'll be in agony ... " Whatever. Be very specific in that way.

We suggest: Once you have done that, fold up the letter and hide it as a symbolic expression of what you usually do with your fear: "I fold it up, and I hide it away." Now you obviously are going to know where it is, but you symbolically hide it.

Bring it out the next day, read it again, and make it stronger. Read it that second time. Make the "sort of's" absolute; the "maybe's," definite. Make it stronger. Then fold it up and hide it again.

The third day you bring it out, and you read it again. Don't skim it. Don't go through it quickly. Read it word for word, and then page by page burn it — safely — in the sink or someplace like that so you don't have to have a fear of fire! Burn the pages, one by one, and sense them being released — a symbolic release of the fear.

As a very specific technique, once you've looked at the loneliness you're really speaking of, and have looked at the love you really don't think you have, and then have written a "fear letter" over a three-day period, you will release the fear through consumption of flame. That will have a very powerful impact upon releasing those fears.

Finally: Look at what the fear is symptomatic of, because every fear is a symptom of something. Find the symptom — the symbolic meaning — and release it. Work with that, and then the fear can be released.

Brian Enright/Lisa Michelle Guest, **Los Angeles &**
Orange County Resources, *Los Angeles*

The Environment: Its Survival

Q My question is concerning two problems that bother the planet right now. One is nuclear proliferation, and the other would be the solid waste and toxic waste problems that bother physical entities. What do you, as a nonphysical entity, suggest that we do about these problems?

Lazaris: All right. Well, certainly so, they are problems in your world, absolutely. The fear of nuclear proliferation is indeed a legitimate concern. First, we would tell you at this point that your world is not going to be destroyed by such activities.

Now that does not mean that everyone should put down their placard, go home, and just forget their protest and their activity. Rather, it means that you're going to win the battle.

Those who are concerned about such issues are making a contribution as they do what they do. And we stress: Some will carry their placards down to City Hall. Others will write letters. Others will spend money. Others will travel in international circles speaking forth to inspire solutions to these problems. All of them, in their own ways, are making a contribution to a future that already has been determined where indeed you're not going to explode yourselves, you're not going to blow yourselves up in that way. This is true not because others are going to prevent it, but because *you* are going to prevent it through negotiations, through communications, through education. This problem is going to be solved more through education than it is through political/bureaucratic negotiations. Now we do not discourage political/bureaucratic negotiations. Absolutely, they're a part of the answer. A bigger part of the answer is going to be:

One: Education. People will be learning about the real dangers, the real threats, the real concerns.

Two: The solution is going to be coming from people who are willing to see that there can be a solution, who are willing to say, "Yes, I believe, although I don't know what it is yet, that there is a solution out there, and I'm going to reach for it, and I'm going to stretch for it, and I'm going to start Dreaming that that reality comes into play."

As you educate, and as you Dream, we suggest that solutions will be found. The solutions will then be picked up by the politicians and the bureaucrats who never really ultimately "lead," but who ultimately "follow." They will then pick up and make official that which you as individuals have decided and that which you, a part of the consensus reality, have decided will be the future.

To find solutions to solid and toxic waste, you need to look at: "What am I really creating here?" Now we know that you as an individual are not directly creating toxic waste or solid waste problems in your world, but you are *allowing* them. Therefore, be personally responsible: "All right, I'm not causing it, but I am allowing it, and therefore, what is this problem speaking to? What am I saying about myself?" Also ask: "What am I saying about my world, about my society, about the humanity of which I'm a part with solid waste and toxic waste problems?"

"As people start valuing themselves and valuing their space — and we mean literally their territory, their space — we suggest that there will come a 'demand' for solution."

What you're saying has to do with your value. As people start valuing themselves and valuing their space — and we mean literally their territory, their space — we suggest that there will come a "demand" for solution. Already, in terms of the solid waste concern, there are already new solutions in the works, new ways of incinerating and working with waste to turn it into energy. You'll see, in the next five to seven years, those solutions becoming more apparent.

As far as toxic wastes are concerned, again we suggest that there will be solutions. Admittedly, it will take a little longer to have a full solution. Toxic waste materials will find their way into recycling processes whereby they will turn again to energy. Through recycling and recycling, the problem, though not eliminated, will at least be put in a perspective. Therefore, it will be approachable and workable and resolvable.

There will be exciting potential solutions which will begin to show themselves in 1988-1989.

Anonymous Question, "The Murray Needleman Show"
WWDB Radio, Philadelphia

Q: As well as the environment, the animals, the wildlife, are in great jeopardy. I'd like you to comment on what we can do to bring about a solution. Is this supposed to happen? Is this part of a natural evolution where we lose so many species? Are we supposed to evolve new species? What is going to happen with wilderness?

Lazaris: With wilderness ... Well, there are those that would want us to put forth what we call a "simple answer" or a "patriotic" answer: "Oh, yes, you have to save everything. Therefore, all the species new and old, all the plants new and old, all the energy has to be maintained."

Some environmentalists, well-meaning and good-hearted and filled with all kinds of love and joy, seek that simplest of answers. "I don't know," they say to themselves. "I don't know which. Should this one survive? Should that one survive? I just don't know, and I would hate to have to play God, and therefore I think I'll just promote the idea that everything should survive."

Many environmentalists are coming to the realization that environment is more complex than that. Ironically, to make a grand sweeping statement is perhaps a limited scope, is perhaps too simplistic a view of how reality works. Therefore, modern or contemporary environmentalists are looking and realizing that perhaps some species of animals, some species of plants, are meant to come and go. As one looks at the history before humankind (and even with humankind before the massive amount of control that humans exerted over Nature), Nature, all on Her own, eliminated certain species of animals and eliminated certain species of plants, etc., and used Her own natural means to experiment, to explore, to bring into being, and take out of being, various living forces.

It is not that you as humans should necessarily decide which ones to keep and which ones not to keep. Rather, it is to open up to the harmony and balance of Nature. Maybe there is a direction. Learn to cooperate with God/Goddess/All That Is to create the appropriate harmony and balance. No, don't play God when it comes to eliminating certain species, but don't play God when it comes to keeping certain ones, either.

You can look at the environmental issues not only throughout the United States, but throughout the world. Perhaps that is what part of the lesson of Chernobyl was all about: You can't just clean up your own environment and think that all of a sudden the world is going to be safe. Just because they closed down the nuclear plant in your neighborhood doesn't mean that they're going to do so around the world. That you can clean up your own environment is indeed a valuable approach — it is the place to begin — but do not fool yourself into thinking that that is all you must do.

Realize that the environment is a complex issue. If you want to, you can find far too many examples to suggest that there's no hope, there's no solution, there are no answers. With the wilderness areas, it can seem "too late." Many are shrugging their shoulders and saying, "It's over." It doesn't have to be that way, though.

The first answer is that you need to stop blaming. Stop blaming somebody else for the problem. Westerners get together and blame the Third World, and the

Third Worlders get together and blame the Westerners and the Easterners. Everybody blames everybody else.

There are conferences — we're oversimplifying it in our answer here — where people spend three-quarters of the time figuring out "who's at fault here," and maybe one-quarter of the time realizing "we need to find a solution," and then everyone goes home.

"No, don't play God when it comes to eliminating certain species, but don't play God when it comes to keeping certain ones, either."

If these groups would stop blaming one another, and stop deciding who's the culprit, and who's the bad guy, and start looking at the fact that "yes, we have a problem and let's start Dreaming the solution" — then solutions will be found.

The second answer is to start Dreaming. We use a capital "D" on the word Dreaming, because we're not speaking of getting daydreamy, or just wishfully thinking. We're suggesting that you start Dreaming — Dreaming of solutions, Dreaming of answers, deciding what world you want to have. Make the decision as to what the world should look like in five years, in 10 years — at least your world personally, if not the world-at-large.

This is evidenced already. For many months we have encouraged Dreaming and Visioning. As people, individuals like you and your friends, start Dreaming — not waiting for the officials, not waiting for your bureaucrats — solutions can be found. Start Dreaming. Stop blaming and start Dreaming. And as others around you stop blaming and start Dreaming, stop blaming and start Dreaming, it grows, it grows. Solutions can be found.

Case in point: the deforestation problem. For the first time in 10 years there is optimism. There have been conferences of the dignitaries, the "men of the world," and some women for that matter, who are from the forest-producing nations and from the forest-using nations. For 10 years they have bickered. For 10 years they have blamed. For 10 years they've met, and they've gotten nowhere. In 1987 for the first time, they've gotten somewhere. For the first time there is definite optimistic progress being made in the reforesting process. The progress was not to stop people from cutting down trees, but to teach them how to cut them down more effectively and to teach them how to replace them much more quickly. There is hope now like there never has been before.

Therefore, the assumption that all the forests are going to be gone, which might have been true in March, in April, 1987, is now different. That process has begun. Certainly it's not the final answer, but what happened there is just what we are suggesting here: that people stopped blaming and they started Dreaming, and out of their Dreaming they came up with at least beginning solutions, at least the first steps toward reforesting and toward saving the existing forests.

It's a beginning that can expand, and it is going to spread into other areas of the environment. Not every species will be saved. There will be those that will be tragically lost and never recovered.

Release that part of yourselves that wants to find out "who did this to me," and start realizing you have to pull together to create what we call a "synergy of decision-making" where indeed each party contributes something, and the whole that is created — the ultimate decision, the ultimate policy — is greater than any sum of the parts. As that starts happening, solutions — simple ones, more complex ones, and then more intricate ones — are ultimately going to be found.

"Stop blaming and start dreaming."

The environment will suffer, but it will not be destroyed. Wilderness will be appreciated, and will come back. The balance between animals and wilderness will similarly prosper and flourish. As cynical as you can become in your world, thinking that no one really cares about the gentleness of a flower (and we suggest it can look that way), when it comes right down to it, yes, you do care. You, as a human consciousness, do care and will make the difference. You will change the direction of the future. The world and its environment will be a whole lot better than the cynical part of each person would imagine it would be.

The Positive Future

Q: Edgar Cayce made the comment at one point that the Soviet Union indeed would turn things around and save the world from nuclear destruction. Can you make a comment on that? What can we do to actively participate in these solutions without being part of the chaos?

Lazaris: To the extent that there is a relationship between the USA, the USSR and China, we suggest that this relationship will develop over the next number of years. It's not the Soviet Union that's going to save you. And it's not China that's going to save you. Nor is the United States, all alone, going to save you. It is going to be a synergy, a whole that is greater than the sum of the parts, a synergy of cooperation that will evolve between these three worlds.

Americans have a particular nature about them, as a whole. As a people you tend to put yourselves down. You tend to be supercritical of yourselves. If there's something wrong, "it's our fault." If there's something right, "it's their doing."

This is a quality of the American that is on one hand endearing, and on the other hand is very sad. No, you are not going to be the destructors of the world, nor is the Soviet Union going to be the savior. You as a consciousness, as a human consciousness, as a country, will reach and stretch and grow and will be very instrumental in the survival of the planet, as will the Soviet

Union. As bridges are now being built between the two, Mainland China will also participate. If you're wise you'll start building bridges from the United States to China. The last linkup will indeed be between the Soviet Union and China. Ironically, that link will be the most difficult.

When that connection is made there will not be world government, nor one monetary system, nor one banking system. Definitely not. Rather, there will be a cooperation where the decision will be made: This world must survive.

With the heart, with the love, and with the forgiveness that is so much a part of America, and with the persistence that is so much a part of Europe and Asia, together you will produce the results that you're looking for. Though we do not suggest a utopic future where you can just sit back and twiddle your thumbs, we see a positive future where you are going to be the creators, where you as people more than as governments are going to pull together. Rather than governments deciding policy and people complying, you — people — will decide and governments will comply. It's there, whenever, wherever you are ready.

*Victoria Fugit, **The Catalyst**, Salt Lake City*

Q: Some speak of the coming Christ, a Maitreya, a world leader. Can you speculate on the coming of such a Messiah?

Lazaris: Well, you know, there is the whole *Book of Revelation* which speaks of that Second Coming, certainly so. And many in the metaphysical community — not wanting to be left out — have created their own sort of "revelatory dream." It's called Doom and Gloom. It's called The End of Time. It's called The Coming of the Great Masters. By whatever name, it matters not. In fact, the Christian revelations and the New Spirituality of the New Age are a personal and private experience.

In that same Bible that speaks of the revelations, Jesus was asked, "When will you come again? When will you return?" And he says, "Dear woman (as he's speaking to a woman), do not get pregnant, for I shall return before that birth would occur." According to all calculations (in your world, at least), that would be within nine months. Obviously, he was either not telling the truth, or you don't fully understand what the *Book of Revelation* means. We suggest the latter.

Indeed, for each person the first coming of the Christ Consciousness, be it Jesus, Maitreya, Buddha, or whomever, by whatever name you call this incredible love that is the Christ Consciousness, has already happened. It happened in your history as an external event.

The Second Coming, however, is inside of you. It is inside of each person. Each of you comes to that second realization of love on your own. Privately, you come to the recognition of that love within you at your own pace, at your own time, and truly it is a revelation.

Truly it is a time of the coming of the "Masters." It is a time of the selfhood of mastery. Therefore, as far as an event out there in the world occuring on a specific date or dates, no. The New Age does not begin at a certain time on a certain date, nor will the revelations occur in that way, nor will the end or the beginning of the planet occur on a particular date. The Fundamentalist revelations and the metaphysical New Age will happen, but they will happen within. Absolutely. It will happen within because it is a personal process of growth that is happening in a personal universe that you are living in and that you are creating.

Any additional coming of a messiah will happen subjectively, not objectively.

Lazaris: All right, as again we say, it's an individual reality. Indeed, the world is heading wherever you want it to head, where you — not "you" as a collective, but you as the individual — want this world to go.

Q: Could you talk to me about where you think this world's headed?

For some — and we will say a minority — it is heading right down the tubes, to put it in your vernacular. Some are going to create chaos and disaster and all kinds of misery, because that's what they're heaping upon themselves, that's what they're expecting, that's what they're looking for. You do create what you want the most and what you fear the most.

For the majority of you, however, there will be a reality that will indeed get very scary. It'll look like everything's going to cave in. It'll look like a Chicken Little reality where indeed "the sky is falling, the sky is falling."

There will be solutions to the solutionless problems. And you will cause or allow these solutions. There will be results and answers to those questions that seem unanswerable. You will cause or allow these answers.

"... those who were hiding their heads waiting for it to collapse will realize that it does not collapse. They will peek out from under their hiding places and sort of giggle at themselves ... their lives will once again flourish."

There will be those particular energies which will turn around the problems of the world — economic changes that will occur, due to the developments in Japan and in West Germany. These two powers will step in to assist with the burdens of the economic world and will be, in that sense, a source of salvation. You will create a reality in which, ironically, the two nations that tried to "destroy" the world in the '40s will step in to "save the world" in the '90s.

We suggest here that it will get bleak, yes. It will get frightening, yes. But that bleakness and fear will represent the darkness before the dawn. There will be difficulty before the joy.

We suggest that your world is moving into a most incredible time. By the early 1990s you'll know very clearly and very concisely that all this Doom and Gloom and all the horror happened in a microcosmic way, on a scaled-down version, but the world as a whole will indeed be in a much stronger, a much more powerful, and a much more unified and peaceful place than ever. You'll start seeing that in about 1992 or 1993, in this century yet!

At the turn of the century, those who were hiding their heads waiting for it to collapse will realize that it does not collapse. They will peek out from under their hiding places and sort of giggle at themselves and laugh and say, "I knew it wasn't going to be destroyed anyway." Then they'll get back to the business of living, and their lives will once again flourish.

Your life will flourish. It will be a time not of Doom and Gloom, but of new bloom. You're moving into a good period of time — not a perfect one (still people will have problems) — but it won't be the devastation that so many fear, either predictively or suggestively.

"The Complete Guide to Channeling" (video tape)
Penny Price Productions, Pacific Palisades, California

Dreaming the Future

Lazaris: In the future some will opt for "Doom and Gloom" — some will opt for the stresses that life can bring — and others will opt for much more positive, much more powerful, much more exciting realities. Each group will be able to see the other.

Q: Do we really have a choice? Can we really change the future?

In other words, if you choose an exciting, positive, powerful reality, you may also notice other people whose lives seem to be hanging on by a thread, whose lives seem to be "going down the tubes," as the term is put.

They will see you as well. We would point out that you will have the opportunity either to stand strong as an inspiration, as a light, or to knuckle under and fall into the fear. We would encourage the former, quite clearly!

We use this little analogy. Here is a little story about you. You are walking along, and you hear a voice very faintly yelling, "Help!" You're not sure if you really heard anything at all. It might have been the wind or the creak of an old branch that just made a noise. But no, you hear it too consistently. "Help." You hear a faint little sound. "Help, help!"

So you leave your path, and you go looking around, and you find, alas, a person that has fallen down into a well, of all strange things. They're way down at the bottom of a well — the person can't possibly get out — and they are screaming for help as loud as they can.

As you stand up at the top looking in, you have two choices: You can either throw a rope down and lift the person out of the well, and in that sense be an inspiration, be a reason to begin again, be a point in a process of growth, or you can jump down into the well with them. Now there are two of you yelling. Someone's bound to hear!

People have been spending too many years jumping down into the well. There are so many down in the well now that the voices are very loud — very, very loud indeed. Your world is crying forth: "Help! Help! Help!"

Now you have to decide: Are you going to jump down into the well and be one more voice among all those screaming "Help!"? Or are you going to stand strong, stand perhaps alone even, but stand strong and be an inspiration? Are you going to throw them a rope — give them reason to lift out of the pits of their own creation — and to get back onto the solid ground?

You choose.

Brian Williams, The Unicorn, Brisbane, Australia

*This is an article written for **Body, Mind & Spirit Magazine** and published in May of 1987.*

Why Dream?

It has never been clearer and more provable: You create your own reality. Mystics, by whatever definition, have been saying this for centuries, and now your scientists are concluding: Reality is a product of your thought. The specific theories may vary. The conclusions are the same.

The explanations scientists are discovering are the same as the understandings the mystics have been revealing since the beginning of time. The physical and the metaphysical overlap: You create your own reality.

A product of what you observe or what you imagine, reality is an illusion. To some, reality is made up of electrons and protons which function in a totally unpredictable realm of probability; to others, it is made up of "consciousness units" which function in the wondrously luminous realm of possibility. All agree that each person is a participant in the reality experienced — in the reality created.

The Reality

The reality you create is made of raw materials. Those raw materials are crafted and shaped with the tools of manifestation. The blueprint of your reality dictates the design, and the result is the physical representation of your vision.

Choice and decision are the first two raw materials. We would suggest that choice is the first gift from God/Goddess/All That Is. Choice is the seed of decision. Decision is the first step on your Journey Home. Out of your choices and decisions come the thoughts you think and the emotions you feel. These are additionally the raw materials of manifestation. Remaining are the attitudes with which you view the illusion and the beliefs that ultimately govern the illusion. These six elements are the raw materials from which you carve your reality.

The pivotal raw materials are both choice and belief. As you exercise the gift of choice, you potentially alter or at least influence all the other raw materials of manifestation. Similarly, as you change your beliefs, all the other components shift. If choice and belief remain unchanged, all other raw materials stagnate. Reality remains in a state of inertia.

Inertia is a state of rest or motion that remains unchanged until there is a force that is equal to or greater than it to change it. The force that is equal to or greater than the existing pattern of reality is choice and belief.

The Tools of Manifestation

To create your reality, you need more than raw materials. You need to skillfully develop the tools of manifestation, the tools of creation. You must discover the tools and learn how to use them. Developing the skill of creation or improving your ability to create is another way of discovering and developing your personal power. Everyone creates their own reality. Some do it more creatively and skillfully — more elegantly — than others. The difference: Do you constructively and imaginatively use the tools of manifestation? The terms *tools of manifestation* and *tools of creation* sound as though they should be very complicated and complex. In fact, they are disarmingly simple. There are only three of them with which each of you creates your entire reality. With these three powerful tools you sculpt an illusion you call your reality.

Desire is the first tool of manifestation or creation. Spoken or unspoken, overt or covert, all creation begins with desire. Expectation follows. Once you desire something, it is critical to creation that you actually expect that something to happen. Expectancies often seem automatic. Look at any positive reality creation and on some level of consciousness, you did expect it.

Beyond, yet mingled with desire and expectation, the final tool of reality creation is imagination. Your imaginings breathe life into the otherwise wishful thinking of your desires and the otherwise fanciful whims of your expectations.

You might say there is a wonderful alchemy that takes place when you combine these three magical ingredients. With a delightful mixture of desire, expectancy, and imagination, the choices and decisions, the thoughts and feelings, and the attitudes and beliefs become dense and massive. They become your physical reality.

A spectacular synergy, where the whole is much more than the sum of the parts, occurs. The parts (the raw materials), when chiseled, carved, sculpted, and conjured by the intricacy and intimacy of your personal desires and private expectations, are lifted into manifestation by the power and awe of your imagination. By the merging and mingling of the tools, the raw materials come alive.

The Secret of Dreaming

Where do you get your desires? What is the origin of your expectancy and your imagination? The tools seem so much a part of you that you seldom consider their source. The tools of manifestation come from your dreams. Your night dreams do generate desire, expectation, and imagination. But an even richer source is the Dream of the Future

— the hope and the stretch of probability, and the reach of possibility — the Dream (with a capital "D") of the Future.

The more you Dream, the greater desire, expectancy, and imagination you have. The more you Dream, the more constructively and uniquely you will use the desires, expectancies, and imaginings you already have.

Don't you see? Whenever something is created something else is lost. When you manifest something in your reality, a certain part of your desire is lost. A piece of your expectancy is gone. Something of your imagination is given up. Once you have something, whether that something is tangible or abstract, you do not desire it or expect it — you have it. You no longer imagine what it would be like to have whatever "it" is — you know now. Whenever something is created, some of the tools of creation are lost. That is the price of creating your own reality.

It is a price well worth paying. As long as you Dream you have unlimited desire, expectation, and imagination — as long as you Dream, that is. The way you replenish the lost desire, expectancy, and imagination is by Dreaming. The tools that get used up in the process of creating get replaced by the process of Dreaming.

The Problem

The problem: Your world is telling you to stop Dreaming. The Way of the World — the Mass Consciousness — is encouraging you to give up on your Dreams. You are told to be more "realistic" in this harsh world of yours. You are told not to be so foolish as to think your Dreams can come true. You are told to stop — stop Dreaming.

The admonitions go further. The Mass Consciousness further entreats you to drop desire, for it is selfish — and to lower or eliminate your expectations and accept whatever happens as okay and not to waste your time imagining, for it will get you nowhere.

Many have already given up their desires, expectations, and imaginings. Many have already stopped Dreaming. Many more will. Without Dreams and the desire, expectancy, and imagination they spawn, you do not have the tools necessary to consciously create your own reality. You will still create it, but you will have to rely on the way of the world. You will have to rely on the Mass Consciousness. Without your own Dreams and what comes with them, you will relinquish your creativity and your power to create what you want. You will feel out of control. You will listlessly accept whatever the world dishes out to you. You will be a sheep.

The More Serious Problem

In the non-metaphysical world, this problem and these admonitions are not new. You as metaphysicians are well used to this diatribe. There is a more serious problem, however. Now many so-called spiritual leaders and teachers (who refuse to call themselves leaders and teachers) are similarly telling you to stop your Dreams and to lay down your desire, expectancy, and imagination.

When the attack comes from without, you can handle it. When the attack comes from within, however, you are often unprepared to deal with the confusion. You are often unwilling to deal with the discernment that is necessary. Discernment is now popularly called "judgment" by the non-leader leaders and the non-teacher teachers.

When the attack comes from within, it often comes cloaked in subtlety. The words are often there, but the understanding and the meaning are missing.

Those who want you to stop Dreaming *say* you create your own reality, and they similarly tell you that there is a

God and/or Goddess who loves you. They are very ready — we would suggest almost too ready — to tell you how very much they themselves really love you. The words are correct, but the meaning is missing.

You are first told you create your own reality. Then you are told that the world is coming to an end or is going through some vaguely abstract, but very destructive, purging/healing process about which you can do nothing. The obvious contradiction is assuaged by abandoning the power to create your own reality. The abandonment is augmented by the short-sighted opinion that the romance and adventure of attempting to endure the impending doom is more exhilarating than the "humdrum" of taking responsibility for a daily reality.

Imagine someone with a 15-year-old son with pink hair and a safety pin in his cheek, a 17-year-old daughter whom they hope is just putting on weight (rather than being pregnant), and bills that accrue faster than paychecks. For many, it is more fun to contemplate an easy end to those problems, even if it means the world is destroyed. It is more romantic and exciting to plan how they are going to endure the elements than it is to take a serious look at the reality they are creating. Also, when solutions are not readily available, those of limited thought and limited vision assume there are no solutions.

Many of the non-teacher teachers *say* they create their own reality, but they do not believe it. *They* cannot see solutions to the many personal and world problems, so they assume there are no solutions. Sadly, it is their truth that they end up "non-teaching" to those who have come to them for insight.

The non-teachers claim that what they teach is only their truth. Therefore, when someone eager to learn — someone who is paying money to be "non-taught" — listens and believes, without questioning the contradictions and without attempting to discern, it is indeed the reality that *they*, not the non-teacher, have created. We do not judge the non-teachers; we merely observe them.

What Happens Then: The Price

The result is that you forget that you create your own reality. You forget that all solutions to all problems have always and will always lie in the midst of or at the end of a Dream. You forget to Dream.

It is very popular in the metaphysical community to gather meteorological and geological data, which is at best highly speculative, and add a few mystical phrases to produce instant prophesy. It is also very popular to research ancient teachings written before people knew they created their own reality and combine the archaic with the instant to produce a prophesy of Doom and Gloom.

The problem with such an approach is not whether you are going to live or die — you have done both so many times already. The problem is that to accept these inevitabilities requires not only that you forget that you create your own reality: You must also forget to Dream.

There is another price to pay. You must also forget that there is a God who cares. It is often said you cannot do anything about the Doom and Gloom, because the Earth must purge itself, and the Earth does not care about you. Even if you want to pretend the Earth does not care, God does care. When you accept the inevitability of doom, you close the door to a caring God/Goddess/All That Is.

The Solution: Shimmering Possibility

We distinguish, and encourage you to distinguish, between sincere concern and Doom and Gloom. Sincere concern may point out impending problems and then will offer sincere methods and techniques not just to escape the path of doom, but actually to re-create the reality so as to eliminate the dangers. Doom and Gloom will talk of the same concerns — often exaggerated to create panic — and will, at best, tell you where to hide and, at worst, tell you there is no place to hide. They will leave you with a hopeless inevitability rather than a shimmering possibility.

Those who offer Doom and Gloom, similarly, have lost sight of a God that is real. They have lost sight, in their limited vision and in their limited thought, of a God by any name that exists beyond them and their human limitations. They honestly think that *they* are All That Is! They pass on their limitations to those who will listen through the subtlety of their own Doom and Gloom — through their own dimly lit reality.

The Dream

It is time to start Dreaming again. It is time to awaken the desire and the expectation of a glorious reality filled with love and laughter. It is time, more than ever, to call forth your imagination to breathe life once again into the Dreams you have dutifully put aside.

Through your desires, expectancies, and imaginings you will begin to Dream. Through your Dreams, you will awaken the desire, expectations, and imagination so critical in reality creation. You will once again have the tools necessary to consciously create your own reality.

It is time to awaken that spark of love that is within each of you. You are the Hope of the Future. You are the Inspiration of Humankind. Some people will create a world that does not seem to care. Others, using their Power of Dominion — their power to create a friendly world — will create a loving world that seems to care a great deal. Does the world care about you or not? You can speculate and argue this point forever. The real point is: You do care about the world! That is an issue you can answer now.

It is imperative that you start Dreaming again. Within the Dreams lie the solutions to all the problems in your reality. Society tells you to stop Dreaming when there are so many problems to solve, when that is precisely the time to start. Within the Dreams that each of you dreams lies the new vista of creativity; within the Dreams that each of you dreams lie the farthest stretches of your personal vision.

Through the Dream you discover a lost power, the power of knowing that there is a God/Goddess/All That Is and that you are loved by that Source of All. When you stop Dreaming, you also stop letting the love in. You stop believing that you are love — you stop believing that you can love.

You are loved. You do love. You love so beautifully. You need to rediscover through your Dreams so that you might begin to glimpse the profound joy and serenity that that love provides.

Wake up and Dream. Wake up and more consciously create your reality. Wake up and love and let yourself be loved.

With love and peace ...

Lazaris

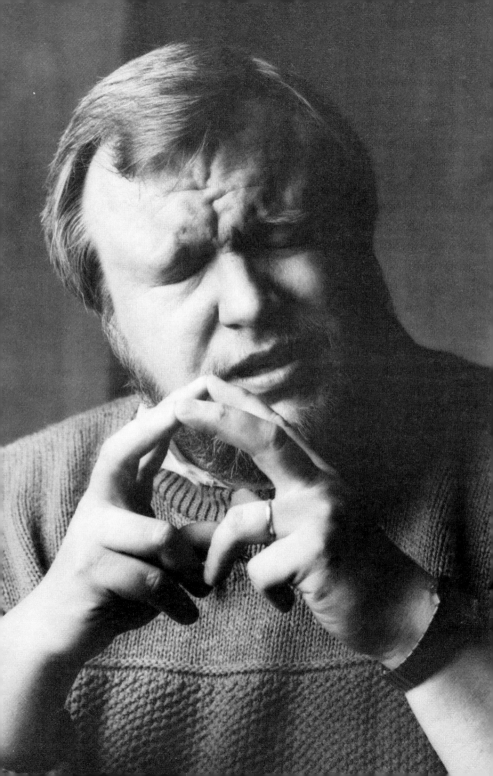

Appendix

More Information about Lazaris ...

Lazaris regularly conducts evening, one-day and weekend workshops (and sometimes seminars that are four days or longer) on an ever-expanding variety of topics. You will find a description of some of these on the next page. Lazaris visits many major American cities each year. A partial list of those cities includes Los Angeles, San Francisco, Atlanta, New Orleans, Seattle, Houston, Miami, Boston, Chicago, Philadelphia & Tampa.

Private consultations with Lazaris are available, though they cannot be guaranteed due to the number of people requesting them. If you would like to request a reading, please write to Concept: Synergy at the address below and ask us to send you a "Consultation Request Form."

If you would like to be placed on Lazaris' mailing list and be notified of workshops and seminars, please call or write us at:

Concept: Synergy, 279 S. Beverly Drive, Suite 604
Beverly Hills, CA 90212
213/285-1507 or 714/337-0789.

Lazaris Seminars

Since October, 1974, when Lazaris began channeling through, he has been constantly and consistently working with people to help them regain their personal power and to guide and befriend them on their Spiritual Journey Home. He has, over the last 14 years, given thousands of personal consultations, and produced dozens of magnificent audio and video tapes (see the following pages for a list of tapes). He also provides an incredibly special experience of growth, empowerment and love through the numerous seminars he conducts.

Evenings with Lazaris *are monthly seminars given in Los Angeles and San Francisco, and once or twice a year in various other cities across the United States. Each month the topic is different as Lazaris continues to unfold the pathway to greater personal freedom and deeper personal ·spirituality. Over the years, Lazaris has covered an amazing array of topics, giving both understanding of how to deal with aspects of personal growth and techniques to move forward into ever-increasing levels of self-love and personal power. Many of these are available now on tape. Each Evening with Lazaris is 3-1/2 hours long and will include both a meditation and a Blending. The taped versions include all of the material of the Evenings except the Blendings.*

Weekends with Lazaris *have been described as "quantum leap" experiences. They are deeply enriching and enabling, a time to move powerfully forward in growth and to gain a far deeper experience of our true selves, our Unseen Friends, our Higher Self, and God/Goddess/All That Is. The information given by Lazaris is profound, and there are always several very deep meditations. Sometimes Weekends with Lazaris incorporate a One-Day Workshop with Lazaris. The Weekends and One-Days are recorded for copyrighting purposes; however, the tapes have not been released for sale.*

Longer Seminars with Lazaris. Over the past several years Lazaris has done several workshops that have been from four to five days long. The first of these was **Realizing Lemuria**, a five-day seminar which was available in 1987. **The Intensive** is a series of seminars, each with a different topic, that are available in 1988 in June, August and October. They are from two to four days long, depending upon the seminar. The Intensive may or may not be available in future years.

For complete information on Lazaris seminars, please contact Concept: Synergy (213/285-1507). We will be glad to provide you with a full list of workshops and seminars.

Channel Jach Pursel ...

Jach Pursel, Lazaris' only channel, was born and raised in Michigan and was graduated from the University of Michigan with a degree in political science in 1969. When Lazaris came through in 1974, Jach was living in Florida and was, as he says, "climbing the corporate ladder," pursuing a career as a business executive for a national company.

Jach Pursel now spends about 30 hours per week channeling Lazaris for private consultations as well as seminars and workshops. In addition, he is Vice President of Isis Rising and Illuminarium Gallery (art galleries), Visionary Publishing, Inc., (an art publishing company) and FutureVision (an investment company). He resides in Beverly Hills, where Isis Rising is located at One Rodeo Drive.

Lazaris VideoTapes

Each of these Lazaris videos is available in VHS, Beta, and PAL. Each tape is two hours long. Cost: $59.95 plus shipping and sales tax if you live in California. There are order forms on the last pages of this book.

Awakening the Love
This tape includes an introduction to Lazaris. Lazaris beautifully and clearly explores "What is Love" and "How to Love Yourself More."

Forgiving Yourself
Spiritual growth begins with self-love and self-forgiveness. Lazaris examines these integral components of The Journey Home.

The Secrets of Manifesting What You Want I
Lazaris discusses several specific programming techniques, including his "33-Second Technique." In meditation we journey to the Causal Plane where programming is intensified.

The Secrets of Manifesting What You Want II
Lazaris moves beyond the necessary tools and materials of creation into the wondrous mysteries and secrets that underlie creating your own reality. Two 33-Second Techniques are included in the final meditation.

Personal Power & Beyond ...
Lazaris explores the core ingredients of Personal Power. Beyond lies the wondrous World of Dominion.

Achieving Intimacy & Loving Relationships
How to create and expand intimacy; how to discover and increase all kinds of loving relationships (not only romantic ones).

Unconditional Love
How to honestly unfold the beauty and the power of the love that is unconditional. Includes a guided meditation.

Releasing Negative Ego
How to distinguish between positive and negative ego. How to elegantly release the negative ego while you develop a positive ego. Includes a transformative meditation.

Unlocking the Power of Changing Your Life

Goes beyond Manifesting What You Want to changing what you already have. Includes the Power of Choice, Power of Image, and a fantastic Change Process.

Spiritual Mastery: The Journey Begins

An exhilarating exploration of each step of our Spiritual Journey. Includes a powerful guided meditation.

Personal Excellence

An in-depth exploration of elegance and excellence — a fundamental step in the Journey Home. Concludes with a powerful meditation.

Developing a Relationship with Your Higher Self

Discover the love between you and your Higher Self. With a magnificent meditation.

The Mysteries of Empowerment

Through discussion and meditation gain the permission and authority to be powerful. Empowerment is a profound mystery of spiritual growth.

The Future: How To Create It

The future: It is filled either with the darkness of fear and inevitabilities or with the shimmer of love and possibilities. Discover how to create the future you want. Includes a beautiful meditation.

Overcoming Fear of Success

More than ever we are ready to deal directly with our fear of succeeding. Lazaris offers liberating understanding and technique.

Developing Self-Confidence

In this tape Lazaris deals with Self-Confidence from a personal and global viewpoint. The whole world is watching and waiting for us to rebuild — to heal — confidence.

Listening to the Whispers

If you listen to the whispers, you don't have to hear the shouts. A fascinating discussion of how to use your reality as gentle feedback for your evaluation.

Personal Growth Tapes

The following cassettes are 3 to 3-1/2 hours long with meditations and are taken from the Evenings with Lazaris over the past few years. Cost of each is $24.95 plus shipping and handling, and sales tax for California residents.

Healing: The Nature of Health I
Healing: The Nature of Health II
The Secrets of Spirituality I
The Secrets of Spirituality II
Loving
Being Loved
Crystals: The Power & Use
Busting & Building Ego
Programming What You Want
The Crisis of Martyrhood
Intimacy
The Magick of Relationships
Earth Energy/Earth Power
The Unseen Friends
Busting & Building Image
Consciously Creating Success
Responsibility & Freedom
Excellence
The Tapestry of Success
The Power of Dominion
Positive Ambition
Gratitude
The Mysterious Power of Chakras
Ending Guilt

The Secrets of Manifesting What
   You Want I
Fear: The Internal War
Discovering Your Subconscious
   With Love & Peace
Developing Self-Confidence
Conquering Fear
Ending Self-Punishment
Ending Self-Sabotage
Harmony: The Power Vortex
Freedom: Its Mystery & Power
Balance: Releasing the Full Self
Abundance: The Skill
The Elegance of Abundance
A Private Consultation
Inner Peace
1988: The Year of Compassion
Lazaris Talks about AIDS at the
   Hay House
Self-Esteem
Self-Worth & Self-Respect
I Deserve!
The Ultimate Relationship
Your Future Self

Books

The Sacred Journey: You and Your Higher Self

The Higher Self ... to reach it, to touch it, to have it touch back has been the dream of spiritual seekers for millenia ... Lazaris lays out a path that leads to the Higher Self, a path of certainty and confidence and preparation that leads to the experience that when you touch your Higher Self, and it touches back, it is real ... $9.95 plus shipping/handling (and sales tax for California residents)

Lazaris Interviews: Book I

Beautiful and elucidating answers to questions on Channeling & The New Spirituality, Women, Men & Sexuality, Discovering God/Goddess/All That Is, Health & Disease, Creating Reality, and a wonderful section called "Lazaris Explains Lazaris." $9.95 plus shipping/handling (and sales tax for California residents).

Lazaris Audio Cassette Tapes

Lazaris Discussions

On Releasing Anger/On Releasing Self-Pity $29.95
On Releasing Guilt/On Receiving Love $29.95
Healing & Releasing Hurt/The Keys of Happiness $29.95

The Red Label Series (Meditations) $29.95 each.

Reducing Fear & Worry/Reducing Stress
Self-Confidence/Self-Awareness
High Energy/Enthusiasm
Happiness/Peace
Reduced Sleep/Improved Sleep
Personal Power/Power & Dominion
Productivity/Impeccability
Improved Health/Balance & Harmony

Other Meditations

Cleaning Chakras/Pituitary-Pineal Meditation $19.95
Beyond the Threshold/Editing the Film $19.95
The Goddess Series I $29.95
The Goddess Series II $29.95
Handling Menstruation $29.95

Lazaris & Peny Tapes $14.95

April 1986 Evening with Lazaris & Peny
July 1986 Evening with Lazaris & Peny
November 1986 Evening with Lazaris & Peny
San Francisco March 1987 Evening with Lazaris & Peny
Los Angeles March 1987 Evening with Lazaris & Peny

Lazaris - Gilbert Williams Calendars $14.95

"For as long as there is Light,
we will love you…"

— *Lazaris*

LAZARIS TAPES
ORDER FORM

_____

NAME

_____

ADDRESS

_____

CITY - STATE - ZIP

_____

PHONE #

☐ *PLEASE ADD MY NAME TO THE MAILING LIST:*

Qty.	Tape Title	Price

VISA, MASTERCARD, AMEX, Accepted	*Money Order &* *Charge Card orders* *shipped within 1 week,* *CA checks held 7 days*	**SUBTOTAL**	
_____ *Charge Card Number-Exp. Date*	*out-of-state checks held* *21 days*	*6.5% Tax* *CA Res.*	
		5% Postage *15% overseas*	
_____ *Signature*	*10.00 charge for* *returned checks*	*($1.00 Minimum)* **TOTAL**	

CONCEPT: SYNERGY

213/285-1500

279 S. Beverly Dr.
Suite 604
Beverly Hills, CA 90212

LAZARIS INTERVIEWS, BOOK II

LAZARIS TAPES ORDER FORM

_____

NAME

_____

ADDRESS

_____

CITY - STATE - ZIP

_____

PHONE #

☐ PLEASE ADD MY NAME TO THE MAILING LIST:

Qty.	Tape Title	Price

VISA, MASTERCARD, AMEX, Accepted

_____

Charge Card Number-Exp. Date

_____

Signature

Money Order &
Charge Card orders
shipped within 1 week,
CA checks held 7 days
out-of-state checks held
21 days

10.00 charge for
returned checks

SUBTOTAL	
6.5% Tax CA Res.	
5% Postage 15% overseas	
($1.00 Minimum) TOTAL	

CONCEPT: SYNERGY

213/285-1500

279 S. Beverly Dr.
Suite 604
Beverly Hills, CA 90212

LAZARIS INTERVIEWS, BOOK II

LAZARIS TAPES
ORDER FORM

NAME

ADDRESS

CITY - STATE - ZIP

PHONE #

☐ _PLEASE ADD MY NAME TO THE MAILING LIST:_

Qty.	Tape Title	Price

VISA, MASTERCARD, AMEX, Accepted

Charge Card Number-Exp. Date

Signature

Money Order &
Charge Card orders
shipped within 1 week,
CA checks held 7 days
out-of-state checks held
21 days

10.00 charge for
returned checks

SUBTOTAL	
6.5% Tax CA Res.	
5% Postage 15% overseas	
($1.00 Minimum) TOTAL	

CONCEPT: SYNERGY

213/285-1500

279 S. Beverly Dr.
Suite 604
Beverly Hills, CA 90212

LAZARIS INTERVIEWS, BOOK II

Other Books by Lazaris ...

The Sacred Journey:
You and Your Higher Self

On the Spiritual Journey Home, the pathway Home to God/Goddess/All That Is, there is the sense that we are somehow bigger than we know — that somewhere there is another part of us that is there to guide us, to help us, to love us. It is a part of us that is evolved now, "already there," and there for us.

The search for the Higher Self is a part of the Spiritual Journey Home, a joyous part of the journey, for the Higher Self, in its immense love, power and vulnerability is an invaluable friend and guide ...

In this landmark book of the New Spirituality, Lazaris unfolds the pathway to the Higher Self by giving us an understanding for the New Age and our own spiritual quest, by laying out for us the growth choices we have already made and the ones we will make. Then he takes us through steps of preparation to clear the obstacles from the pathway, and to explain to us what the Higher Self is, how we can communicate with it, and how we can relate to it for the rest of our lives as we develop an invaluable friendship of clarity, beauty, love and true spirituality. Finally, at the end of the journey, we touch and begin to know our Higher Self in a series of three meditations that many have called the most beautiful they have ever known. At the end of the journey we realize that indeed it is but the beginning of another ...

To Order ... please use the order form on the next page.

To Order ...

Please fill out and clip the order form below and send it to

Concept: Synergy
279 S. Beverly Drive, Suite 604,
Beverly Hills, CA 90212.

Name _____

Address _____

City/State/Zip _____

Telephone(s) _____

Send ___ copies of **The Sacred Journey: You and Your Higher Self** @ $9.95 ea. (****California residents MUST add 6.5% tax) + $2.50 postage/handling for the first book. For more than one copy add $1.00 postage/handling for each additional book.

Enclosed is my ___ check (allow 3 wks. for processing) ___ money order

Please bill my charge card: ___ Amex ___ MC ___ Visa

Card Number _____

Exp. Date ____ Signature _____

Lazaris Interviews: Book I

*A marvelous companion book to this volume, **Lazaris Interviews, Book I** is now a national best seller and a gift for everyone who is interested in growth.*

With the same depth, tenderness, and love that Lazaris has answered the questions in this book, he has also answered a number of questions on Channeling, on Women, Men and Sexuality, on Discovering God/Goddess/All That Is, on Creating Reality, and on Health and Disease. Each chapter is enlightening in its perspective and offers clarity and insight on issues that affect everyone's lives and everyone's growth.

*Among the beautiful discussions in **Lazaris Interviews, Book I** are:*

- *An exploration of the Goddess energy, the emergence of feminine energy, and its role in bringing us closer to God/Goddess/All That Is.*

- *A gentle, thorough, and compassionate discussion of AIDS, of the nature of health, and of Alzheimer's disease.*

- *An elucidating discussion of channeling, why it is so prevalent now, its role in the New Age, and the discernment that is important in evaluating channeled information.*

- *An exhilarating discussion of how we create reality and how we can generate success.*

In addition, there is a powerfully beautiful section where Lazaris explains himself, why he is communicating with us, and the purposes he wants to accomplish. There is great wealth of insight in this book, in the depth and beauty of Lazaris' answers. And there is a great feeling of the love that he has for us all ...

To Order ...

Please fill out the form below and mail it to:

Concept: Synergy
279 S. Beverly Drive, Suite 604
Beverly Hills, CA 90212.

Name _____

Address _____

City/State/Zip _____

Telephone(s) _____

Send ___ copies of **Lazaris Interviews: Book I** @ $9.95 ea. (****California residents MUST add 6.5% tax) + $2.50 postage/ handling for the first book. For more than one copy add $1.00 postage/ handling for each additional book.

Enclosed is my ___ check (allow 3 wks. for processing) ___ money order

Please bill my charge card: ___ Amex ___ MC ___ Visa

Card Number _____

Exp. Date ____ Signature _____